GCSE English

A View from the Bridge

by Arthur Miller

If you're studying *A View from the Bridge*, this superb CGP Text Guide has everything you need to score the best possible grades for your GCSE exams.

We've explained the whole play — characters, language, themes, historical background... it's all in here. And because it's a CGP book, everything's written in a chatty style that's easy to understand.

But that's not all. We've also included plenty of practice questions, and there's a whole section of advice on how to plan and structure answers that'll dazzle the examiners!

The Text Guide

CONTENTS

CONTENTS

Published by CGP

Editors:
Emma Crighton
Heather Gregson
Lucy Loveluck
Anthony Muller
Sabrina Robinson

Contributors:
Samantha Bensted
Marian Feeley

With thanks to David Broadbent, Julia Murphy and Nicola Woodfin for the proofreading.

Acknowledgements:

Cover Illustration © Wolfgang Price 2013

With thanks to Mary Evans Picture Library for permission to use the images on pages 1 & 7

With thanks to iStockphoto.com for permission to use the images on pages 2, 3, 32, 47 & 50

With thanks to ArenaPAL for permission to use the images on pages 3, 4, 5, 10, 25 & 49

With thanks to Alamy for permission to use the images on pages 3, 15 & 26

With thanks to TopFoto.co.uk for permission to use the images on pages 3 & 46 © TopFoto

With thanks to Donald Cooper/photostage.co.uk for permission to use the images on pages 3, 5, 11, 13, 14, 17, 21, 22, 23, 29, 30, 31, 36, & 42

With thanks to Photofest for permission to use the images on pages 5, 16, 24, 28 & 38

With thanks to Rex Features for permission to use the images on pages 37 & 41

With thanks to Lebrecht Music & Arts for permission to use the images on pages 12, 27, 40 & 48

With thanks to The Kobal Collection for permission to use the images on pages 1 & 6

Image on page 8 from the comic book 'Is This Tomorrow' published in 1947 by the Catechetical Guild Educational Society of St. Paul, Minnesota. Reproduced under the terms of the Creative Commons Licence http://creativecommons.org/licenses/by/3.0/

ISBN: 978 1 84762 404 8
Printed by Elanders Ltd, Newcastle upon Tyne.
Clipart from Corel®

Introducing 'A View from the Bridge' and Miller

'A View from the Bridge' is about family and honour

- *A View from the Bridge* is a play about an <u>Italian family</u> living in <u>Red Hook</u>, New York, in the <u>1950s</u>.

- In the play, the head of the family <u>betrays</u> two of his relatives by reporting them as <u>illegal immigrants</u>.

- Although the events are <u>fictional</u>, they're based on Miller's <u>own experiences</u> of working at the docks:

Italian Immigrants in New York

1) In the early <u>1950s</u> many Italians came to America for <u>work</u>. A lot of these immigrants settled in <u>New York</u> and got jobs at the <u>docks</u>.

2) Miller witnessed the <u>lives</u> and <u>hardships</u> of these <u>dockworkers</u> and <u>immigrants</u> first-hand.

3) The play is based on a story Miller heard about a dockworker who <u>reported</u> two relatives to the <u>authorities</u> because one of them was in a <u>relationship</u> with the dockworker's <u>niece</u>.

© Mary Evans / Everett Collection

Arthur Miller was punished for not naming names

- In the 1950s, the House Un-American Activities Committee (HUAC), a body set up to investigate <u>radical political groups</u>, accused thousands of people of being <u>communists</u> (see p.8).

- Miller was called up before the HUAC and was told to <u>name anyone</u> he suspected of being <u>communist</u>. Although others gave names, Miller <u>refused</u> to <u>betray</u> his colleagues and so he was <u>punished</u>.

- The HUAC's investigations <u>inspired</u> Miller to explore the theme of <u>betrayal</u> in *A View from the Bridge*.

1915	Born in New York.
1936	Wrote his <u>first play</u>, 'No Villain'.
1952	Miller's friend Elia Kazan was questioned about <u>communist activity</u> by the HUAC. Kazan <u>agreed</u> to give the <u>names</u> of <u>suspected communists</u>.
1956	'A View from the Bridge' opened in London's West End.
1956	Married <u>Marilyn Monroe</u>.
1957	Miller was questioned by the HUAC. He was <u>sentenced</u> to thirty days in prison and wasn't allowed a <u>passport</u>. He was also <u>blacklisted</u> — he wasn't allowed to <u>work</u>.
1958	Miller's conviction was <u>overturned</u>.
2005	Died, aged 89.

© THE KOBAL COLLECTION

Background Information

Red Hook was a slum in Brooklyn, New York

In the 1950s <u>Red Hook</u> was a very poor area on the <u>seaward side</u> of <u>Brooklyn Bridge</u>.
Here are the <u>key locations</u> in the play:

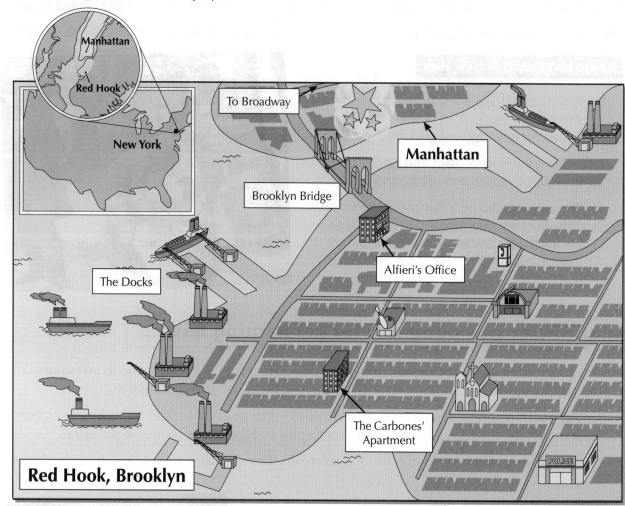

Life in Red Hook was tough

- Red Hook was a popular destination for Italian <u>immigrants</u> as there was a strong <u>Italian community</u>, but it <u>wasn't</u> an <u>easy place to live</u>.

- Many immigrants became <u>dockworkers</u> who unloaded ships, but conditions were <u>poor</u>, there was often a <u>shortage</u> of work and they were <u>badly paid</u>.

- For <u>illegal immigrants</u>, there was the constant <u>fear</u> of being <u>arrested</u> and sent back home.

- In spite of all this, life in Red Hook was still <u>better</u> than <u>life in Italy</u> where there were <u>fewer jobs</u> and <u>no prospects</u>.

Who's Who in Red Hook

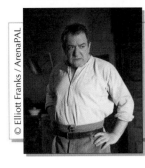

Eddie Carbone...

...is a dockworker. He has brought up Beatrice's niece, Catherine, since she was young, but is starting to have unnatural feelings for her.

Beatrice Carbone...

...is Eddie's wife. They're going through a rough patch, but she still loves him.

Catherine...

...is Eddie and Beatrice's niece. She's nearly eighteen and ready to grow up, but she's still very naive.

Rodolpho...

...is Beatrice's Italian cousin. He comes to America for work, and starts dating Catherine.

Marco...

...is Rodolpho's older brother. He's also come to America for work, to support his family back in Sicily.

Alfieri...

...is a wise lawyer in his fifties. He narrates the events of the play to the audience.

Louis and Mike...

...are dockworkers who live in Red Hook. They are friends with Eddie, and represent the Italian American community.

'A View from the Bridge' — Plot Summary

© Wolfgang Price

'A View from the Bridge'... what happens when?

Here's a little recap of the <u>main events</u> of *A View from the Bridge*. It's a good idea to learn <u>what happens when</u>, so you can show the examiner that you know exactly what you're talking about.

Act One — the cousins arrive

© Elliott Franks / ArenaPAL

- <u>Alfieri</u> explains that he is a <u>lawyer</u> in <u>Red Hook</u>. He tells the audience what life is like there and introduces them to <u>Eddie Carbone</u>. He also reveals that Eddie's story ends <u>badly</u>.

- Eddie is welcomed home from work by his <u>niece</u>, <u>Catherine</u>, and his <u>wife</u>, <u>Beatrice</u>. He tells them that Beatrice's Italian cousins have just <u>arrived in America</u>.

- Beatrice tells Eddie that Catherine has been offered a <u>job</u>. Eddie reluctantly agrees to letting her take it — he isn't ready for her to become <u>independent</u>.

- <u>Marco</u> and <u>Rodolpho</u> arrive at the flat. Catherine shows a <u>romantic interest</u> in Rodolpho.

- Catherine and Rodolpho start dating. After a few weeks, a <u>jealous</u> Eddie tells Catherine that Rodolpho is only interested in her because he wants to be an <u>American citizen</u>.

- Beatrice tells Catherine to start <u>acting</u> like an <u>adult</u> and stop letting Eddie control her life. She warns Catherine to behave <u>appropriately</u> around Eddie.

Act One — Eddie doesn't want to lose Catherine

- Eddie goes to Alfieri for <u>advice</u>. He claims that Rodolpho only wants to marry Catherine so he can <u>legally</u> stay in America. Alfieri says he can't do anything about it, and <u>warns</u> Eddie to control his <u>feelings</u> for Catherine.

- Catherine starts to <u>rebel</u> against Eddie, and <u>openly flirts</u> with Rodolpho in front of him.

- Eddie offers to give Rodolpho a <u>boxing lesson</u>, but he uses the lesson as an <u>excuse</u> to <u>hit him</u>.

- After seeing Eddie <u>hurt</u> his <u>brother</u>, Marco challenges Eddie to a <u>chair-lifting contest</u>.

© Elliott Franks / ArenaPAL

- After Eddie fails, Marco lifts the chair above his head like a <u>weapon</u>. This is a <u>silent warning</u> to Eddie about what will happen if he <u>hurts</u> Rodolpho again.

Act Two — Eddie loses control

- Catherine and Rodolpho are <u>left alone</u> at home for the first time. They talk about getting <u>married</u>.

- Catherine asks him if he'd still marry her if they had to live in <u>Italy</u>. Rodolpho gets <u>angry</u> and says that he wants to <u>marry her</u> *and* <u>live in America</u>. Rodolpho takes Catherine into the <u>bedroom</u>.

- Eddie comes home drunk and <u>catches</u> them coming out of the <u>bedroom</u> — he's <u>furious</u>. He tells Rodolpho to leave the flat.

- Eddie grabs Catherine and <u>kisses</u> her on the <u>lips</u>.

- Rodolpho and Eddie <u>fight</u> and Eddie also <u>kisses</u> him on the <u>lips</u>. He <u>threatens</u> Rodolpho with violence if he doesn't leave.

Act Two — things turn violent

- Eddie pays a second visit to <u>Alfieri</u>, who again <u>warns</u> him not to do anything.

- Despite Alfieri's warnings, Eddie <u>reports</u> Marco and Rodolpho to the Immigration Bureau.

- Eddie learns that Catherine is <u>marrying</u> Rodolpho.

- <u>Immigration</u> officers arrive and <u>arrest</u> Marco, Rodolpho and two other immigrants. Out in the street, Marco <u>accuses</u> Eddie of reporting them. Eddie <u>denies</u> it, but no one believes him.

- Alfieri bails the cousins out of prison. He makes Marco <u>promise</u> he <u>won't hurt</u> Eddie.

- Rodolpho and Catherine get ready for their <u>wedding</u>. Catherine is <u>angry</u> as Eddie won't let Beatrice go.

- Marco arrives and Eddie <u>demands an apology</u> for the accusations Marco made against him.

- Marco <u>refuses</u> to apologise. Eddie and Marco <u>fight</u> — Eddie takes out a <u>knife</u>, but Marco grabs Eddie's arm and makes him <u>stab himself</u>. Eddie <u>dies</u> in <u>Beatrice's arms</u>.

- Alfieri sums up the play. He says that he <u>still loves</u> Eddie despite what he did.

A much better play than 'A View of a Bridge'...

It's not the world's longest play, but it's crammed full of complex characters, tantalising themes and witty writer's techniques. Luckily for you, that's what we're going to spend the next fifty pages looking at. If you're still a bit hazy on the plot, or just want a break from revision, check out the cartoon at the back of the book.

Introduction

Section One — Background and Context

Immigration in 1950s America

Life in Europe in the 1950s was pretty hard — after the Second World War there wasn't enough money, work or food to go around. For some people, it seemed like a good time to start a new life in the good ol' US of A.

Post-war Italy was struggling

1) Italy <u>suffered</u> a lot during WW2 — about 1% of its population were <u>killed</u> (around 450 000 people). A lot of <u>damage</u> was also done to <u>Italian cities</u> and <u>railways</u>. From 1943 onwards, the Allies had used Italy as a base to attack the Germans — the whole country became a <u>battleground</u>.

2) When the war <u>ended</u> in 1945, Italy's <u>economy</u> was <u>devastated</u>:

   - During the war, Italian industry focused on making <u>military equipment</u>.

   - After the war there was <u>less need</u> for things like weapons, so the economy suffered and a lot of people became <u>unemployed</u>. <u>Southern Italy</u> and <u>Sicily</u> (a large island situated to the south of mainland Italy) were particularly affected because they were much <u>poorer</u> than Northern Italy.

   - For many people like Rodolpho and Marco, who were from Sicily, there were <u>no jobs</u> and <u>no prospects</u> — "There's nothing! Nothing, nothing, nothing."

A scene from 'Bicycle Thieves' — a film about Italian poverty after the war.

© PRODUZIONE DE SICA / THE KOBAL COLLECTION

Many Italians saw America as a fresh start

1) <u>American movies</u> were popular all over Europe. These movies encouraged people to believe that <u>America</u> was an <u>exciting place</u> with plenty of <u>opportunities</u>. In Italy, where there was <u>no work</u>, the idea of moving to America was very <u>appealing</u>.

2) The idea of the <u>American Dream</u> became very <u>popular</u>. This was the belief that America was a place where <u>anyone</u> could <u>achieve anything</u>, <u>regardless</u> of their <u>background</u>.

> <u>Rodolpho</u> seems to believe in the <u>American Dream</u>. He says that once he becomes a <u>citizen</u> he "would <u>start</u> to be something <u>wonderful</u>".

Many immigrants came to America illegally

1) Many <u>illegal</u> immigrants that travelled to America came to New York to look for <u>work</u>.

2) There was work in America, but Italian immigrants were often <u>exploited</u>. The gangs who <u>smuggled</u> the immigrants into America found them plenty of (badly paid) work to repay their <u>debts</u>. But when they'd finally cleared their debts, the immigrants had to find their <u>own work</u> — this was often <u>difficult</u>.

3) Some men came to America and left their <u>families</u> behind. They sent back as much money as they could until they could <u>rejoin</u> their family. In the play, Marco comes to America so he can <u>send money back</u> to support his wife and children.

Immigration in 1950s America

New York has five boroughs

1) New York is made up of <u>five boroughs</u> — Manhattan, Brooklyn, Queens, The Bronx and Staten Island.

2) In the 1950s, <u>Manhattan</u> was the <u>wealthiest</u> part of New York, with its <u>theatres</u>, <u>shops</u> and <u>bright lights</u>.

3) The other four boroughs were much <u>poorer</u>, and <u>Brooklyn</u> — the borough where *A View from the Bridge* is set — was perhaps the <u>poorest</u> of them all.

4) When <u>Italians</u> started coming to New York, many chose to live in Brooklyn because there were plenty of <u>cheap-to-rent apartments</u> — Brooklyn was <u>all</u> that they could <u>afford</u>.

The play's title refers to Brooklyn Bridge — the view from the bridge is of Red Hook.

Brooklyn had its own Italian community

1) 1950s Brooklyn was home to the <u>biggest Italian immigrant community</u> in America. This was because:

- Lots of <u>Italian immigrants</u> had <u>already settled</u> in Brooklyn during the <u>1920s</u>. New Italian arrivals preferred to be with people who had a <u>similar cultural background</u>.

- Italian <u>food</u>, <u>music</u> and even <u>churches</u> were available, so Italian immigrants <u>felt at home</u>.

- Italian immigrants tended to <u>look after each other</u> — they <u>felt safe</u> and were probably less worried about being <u>reported</u> to the Immigration Bureau than they would be living elsewhere.

2) Living in an Italian community meant that <u>American life</u> had a limited <u>effect</u> on immigrants. For example, <u>Eddie</u> and <u>Marco</u> still honour the <u>Sicilian code</u> — this was the idea that you dealt with your <u>own problems</u> rather than <u>involving</u> the <u>authorities</u> (e.g. the police and the government).

Life in America was better, but not by much

Despite these conditions, many Italians stayed in America even after earning enough to move away.

1) <u>Dockyard owners</u> encouraged the smuggling of <u>illegal immigrants</u> because illegal immigrants had <u>no rights</u> — they could pay them <u>low wages</u>, and it didn't matter that <u>conditions</u> were <u>poor</u>.

2) <u>Corruption</u> was <u>widespread</u> — the dockyard owners made <u>deals</u> with workers' unions that <u>kept wages low</u>, even though the unions were meant to be looking out for the workers' <u>best interests</u>.

3) Work on the docks was often <u>irregular</u> and <u>unreliable</u> — it depended on how many <u>ships</u> were coming in to dock.

4) Illegal immigrants had <u>no choice</u> but to put up with these conditions because they couldn't get work anywhere else. They weren't <u>legal citizens</u>, so they <u>couldn't complain</u> to anyone, as they could be <u>arrested</u> and sent back home.

A dockyard meeting of a workers' union.

© Mary Evans/Epic / Tallandier

KEY QUOTE

"you'll make better here than you could there."

Marco and Rodolpho don't exactly live a life of luxury in Red Hook, but it's still a darn sight better than their lives in post-war Italy. Their old town didn't have working cars or a pier. War, huh? What is it good for?

Naming Names and McCarthyism

In the 1950s America was scared of communists, and there was a lot of pressure on American citizens to report anyone they suspected of being a communist. This may have inspired Miller to write *A View from the Bridge*.

McCarthyism was a hunt for communists

1) McCarthyism gets its name from the man who started it, <u>Senator Joe McCarthy</u>.

2) During the 1950s, McCarthy campaigned against <u>communism</u>. He was famous for <u>aggressive interrogation</u> and making accusations with <u>little evidence</u>.

3) The <u>HUAC</u> (House Un-American Activities Committee) also questioned many people in <u>Hollywood</u> about <u>communism</u>, including <u>Miller</u>.

4) Many of the people who were accused <u>lost their jobs</u> or were <u>imprisoned</u>. If you were arrested, you were <u>encouraged</u> to <u>accuse</u> others to clear your name.

IS THIS TOMORROW

AMERICA UNDER COMMUNISM!

Communism

- <u>Capitalist</u> societies encourage people to <u>earn their own money</u> in <u>privately owned</u> businesses.

- <u>Communism</u> is the <u>opposite</u> of capitalism. In communist societies everyone is <u>equal</u> (at least in theory) and <u>private ownership</u> doesn't exist.

- Americans were <u>afraid</u> that communist countries, particularly the <u>USSR</u> (which included modern day Russia), were trying to <u>take over the world</u>.

5) <u>Reporting</u> others was used by some for <u>revenge</u> — in a similar way, Eddie reports Rodolpho to the authorities to <u>punish</u> him for his <u>relationship</u> with Catherine.

6) <u>Accusing</u> someone of being a communist <u>ruined</u> their reputation whether it was true or not. This is similar to how Marco's <u>accusations</u> damage Eddie's <u>reputation</u>.

Miller's own experiences influenced 'A View from the Bridge'

1) When Miller was working on the Brooklyn docks, he was actually researching <u>another project</u> — a <u>film</u> which later became *On the Waterfront*.

2) Miller was meant to write the film's <u>screenplay</u> for his friend <u>Elia Kazan</u>. However, Miller <u>left</u> the project when the HUAC put pressure on the filmmakers to make the <u>villains</u> in the film <u>communists</u>.

3) Miller and other important members of the artistic community <u>fell out</u> with Kazan when Kazan agreed to <u>name possible communists</u> for the HUAC. When Miller was asked to do the same, he <u>refused</u>, which meant he was <u>fined</u> and had his passport <u>confiscated</u>.

4) *A View from the Bridge* and *On the Waterfront* can be seen as <u>different interpretations</u> of <u>naming names</u>:

A View from the Bridge

In Miller's play, when Eddie <u>reports</u> Beatrice's cousins to the Immigration Bureau, he's <u>rejected</u> by the community for <u>naming names</u> (much like Kazan was).

On the Waterfront

In Kazan's film, a dockworker (like Eddie), <u>exposes</u> the <u>corruption</u> at the docks. When he <u>names names</u>, he's seen as a <u>hero</u>.

Historical background can tell you more about the play...

Learning about the 1950s will help you to understand *A View from the Bridge* better. For example, Miller's experience with the HUAC helps to explain why honour and reputation are important themes in the play.

Practice Questions

Here's a quick warm-up exercise to see how much knowledge you've absorbed. If the questions prove a bit tricky, read through the section again and have another go, otherwise move ahead to the in-depth questions.

Quick Questions

1) Give two examples of problems in Italy after the war.

2) Explain what is meant by the American Dream in one sentence.

3) Give two reasons why Italian immigrants settled in Brooklyn.

4) Why did illegal immigrants put up with terrible working conditions?

5) What is the main difference between capitalism and communism?

6) Why did Arthur Miller fall out with Elia Kazan?

Write a paragraph or so for each in-depth question — make sure you back up your points with examples.

In-depth Questions

1) Explain why Italians might have chosen to come to America instead of somewhere else.

2) What do we learn about life as an illegal immigrant in 1950s New York from *A View from the Bridge?*

3) To what extent do you think that Miller's own experiences with Kazan and the HUAC inspired the story of *A View from the Bridge*?

Analysis of Act One — Domestic Troubles

So, now you know the general plot of the play, it's time to dive right in... It's like an episode of Jeremy Kyle: "My husband fell for our niece and was then brutally stabbed by her boyfriend's brother" — deep stuff...

Alfieri wants to tell us a story

Theme — Justice

This introduces the themes of justice and conflict.

Alfieri begins the play by talking directly to the <u>audience</u> and he <u>helps set the scene</u>:

- He talks about how <u>gangsters</u> lived and died in the area: "there were many here who were <u>justly shot</u> by <u>unjust</u> men. <u>Justice</u> is very important here."

- He calls Red Hook a "slum" and "the gullet of New York" — it's a <u>tough</u>, <u>working-class</u> neighbourhood.

- He <u>foreshadows</u> the play's events by saying <u>lawyers</u> are "thought of in connection with <u>disasters</u>". As he introduces Eddie's story he claims he was "<u>powerless</u>" and could only watch events run their "<u>bloody course</u>" — a tragic ending is <u>inevitable</u> as the play's events have already happened.

Eddie and Catherine are very close

© Elliott Franks / ArenaPAL

1) Their affection for each other is clear when Catherine greets Eddie <u>warmly</u>. Eddie is *"pleased"* but *"shy about it"* — he's <u>happy</u> but <u>uncomfortable</u> with his <u>feelings</u>.

2) They have a <u>father-daughter</u> relationship:

- Catherine <u>shows</u> Eddie her new skirt in a <u>childlike</u> way — "You like it?"

- Eddie is <u>protective</u> of her, saying her skirt is "<u>too short</u>" and she's "<u>walkin' wavy</u>".

- When Eddie "<u>disapproves</u>" Catherine is *"almost in tears"* — she seeks Eddie's approval as if he was her <u>father</u>.

Eddie and Beatrice are going through a rough patch

1) They seem to have a <u>loving</u> marriage — Eddie is <u>concerned</u> about people taking advantage of Beatrice's 'big heart' and asks her what's wrong when she starts <u>crying</u>.

2) The <u>stage directions</u> also give clues — he *"touches her hand"* to <u>comfort</u> her, they look into each other's eyes and Beatrice <u>holds</u> Eddie's *"face in her hands"*.

3) But, there are also <u>tensions</u> — Beatrice is "<u>afraid</u>" of Eddie, and she gets angry with him when he doesn't want to let Catherine take a stenographer <u>job</u>. She makes him agree to let her work.

4) This shows that Beatrice, like Eddie, is also <u>protective</u> of Catherine. This includes protecting Catherine from <u>Eddie's control</u>, even though Beatrice is <u>scared</u> of how Eddie will react.

Write about the initial atmosphere of the play...

Show that you understand the effect of Alfieri's monologue — there's a sense that something bad is about to happen. No wonder everyone's so stressed — I'm not even there and I think I need a brown paper bag...

Analysis of Act One — Domestic Troubles

The arrival of Marco and Rodolpho is when the action really starts — the house dynamics are shaken up, new relationships form and tensions increase — who needs TV when you've got AVFTB?

The story of Vinny Bolzano is a warning of what's to come

1) Eddie and Beatrice tell the story of Vinny Bolzano who "<u>snitched</u> to the <u>Immigration</u>" about his own <u>uncle</u>. Afterwards, Vinny was <u>beaten</u> by his family, and they "<u>spit</u> on him in the street".

2) The local community were <u>disgusted</u> by the <u>betrayal</u> — this shows how <u>tight-knit</u> their community is and the importance of family <u>loyalty</u>.

3) Vinny's story <u>foreshadows</u> what will later happen to Eddie, after he <u>calls</u> the Immigration Bureau.

4) The story also introduces the idea that "you can <u>quicker</u> get back a <u>million dollars</u>... than a <u>word</u> that you gave away" — perhaps the <u>moral</u> of the play.

Theme — Justice

The Red Hook Italian community believe in taking the <u>law</u> into their <u>own hands</u>.

Beatrice's cousins contrast with each other

Theme — Honour

Eddie considers it "an honor" to <u>help</u> his relatives — even if it is <u>illegal</u>.

Shortly after dinner, Marco and Rodolpho arrive from Italy. It's immediately clear that they are <u>very different</u>:

Rodolpho

- He's <u>small</u>, pale skinned and fair-haired.
- He's chatty and <u>excited</u> to be in America — "This will be the first house I ever walked into in America!"
- He's a <u>dreamer</u> — he talks about hoping to be a motorcycle messenger and wants "to be an American".

Marco

- He's "<u>*square-built*</u>" and <u>dark-skinned</u>.
- Marco is "<u>*quiet-voiced*</u>" and says <u>little</u> — one of his first lines is to shush Rodolpho — "Ssh! Come".
- He's <u>practical</u> and a <u>realist</u>. He's only in America to <u>earn money</u> for his family. He plans to <u>return</u> home in a few years.

Catherine and Rodolpho grow closer

1) It's clear that a <u>relationship</u> will form between the two characters <u>straightaway</u>. Catherine talks to Rodolpho "<u>*wondrously*</u>", is "<u>*enthralled*</u>" by his singing, and is quick to find out if he is married.

2) Rodolpho describes her as "<u>beautiful</u>", and clearly enjoys how much <u>attention</u> she is giving him.

3) Catherine's sexual <u>interest</u> in Rodolpho is suggested by her <u>high-heels</u> — a symbol of her increased <u>sexual awareness</u> (see p.50 for more).

© Donald Cooper/photostage.co.uk

Mention the differences between Marco and Rodolpho...

Marco and Rodolpho really are like chalk and cheese — show that you understand the differences between them. Who will succeed, the practical chalk or the soft cheese? Tune in... er, read the next page to find out.

Analysis of Act One — Domestic Troubles

As Act One continues, everyone's talking about the complicated relationships in the Carbone household. Eddie's the star of the show — he acts like a right drama queen and decides to get the law involved.

Eddie doesn't approve of Catherine's relationship with Rodolpho

1) Eddie watches Rodolpho with "*concealed suspicion*" from the start because he realises Catherine is attracted to him.

2) After they've been dating for a few weeks Eddie is even more agitated — he waits impatiently in the doorway of the building for them to come home from the movies.

3) Eddie complains that Catherine is becoming distracted, "I don't see her practice no more", but it's likely that he's just jealous — as Beatrice suggests.

4) Eddie claims that Rodolpho gives him the "heeby-jeebies". He blames his lack of sexual interest in Beatrice on the cousins' presence, but Beatrice says they haven't been intimate for months.

5) Eddie tries to ruin Catherine and Rodolpho's relationship by telling Catherine that Rodolpho is only interested in her because he wants to become "an American citizen". Catherine refuses to believe him.

Beatrice gives Catherine some advice

1) Beatrice tells Catherine to stop acting "like a baby" and grow up. She tells her not to worry about what Eddie thinks — no man will ever be good enough for her in Eddie's eyes.

2) She also questions how Catherine acts around Eddie, suggesting that she's being unintentionally provocative by walking around in just a "slip" (a thin undergarment worn under dresses and skirts).

3) Beatrice gives Catherine advice because she wants her to be happy, but she also has her own motives. She hints that she's "jealous" of Catherine and implies that Catherine is accidentally responsible for her marital troubles with Eddie.

Eddie visits Alfieri for legal advice

1) Eddie wants to know if the law can stop Rodolpho and Catherine's relationship. However, Alfieri can "only deal in what's provable" and he's powerless to help.

2) Eddie has suspicions about Rodolpho's motives and claims that he "ain't right" (he thinks he's gay) because he can sing and sew.

3) Alfieri tells Eddie the only legal issue surrounding the cousins is the "manner in which they entered the country", but they both realise that Eddie doesn't "want to do anything about that".

> **Theme — Honour**
> Alfieri was born in Italy, so he knows about the Italian code of honour — families stick together.

 "Jesus, no, I wouldn't do nothin' about that"

Eddie's obviously upset about Catherine's relationship with Rodolpho, and he even turns to the law to try to get rid of him. But he won't report the fact that Rodolpho is an illegal immigrant — not yet, anyway...

Analysis of Act One — Domestic Troubles

Ah, yes, the 'lifting a chair above your head' trick — a classic display of strength. No, I've never heard of it either... Marco finally realises that Eddie isn't the honourable guy everyone thinks he is.

Things get more and more tense in the house

1) Eddie <u>interrupts</u> Rodolpho when he speaks, and picks <u>fights</u> with him over petty things like taking Catherine out "without permission".

2) <u>Beatrice</u> seems to be <u>losing patience</u> with Eddie and reminds him to act like "an <u>uncle</u>" — he's being too <u>controlling</u> and acting like a <u>jealous lover</u>.

3) Catherine also starts to <u>stand up to Eddie</u> — she is *"flushed with revolt"* when she asks Rodolpho to <u>dance</u> with her. She knows it will make Eddie <u>angry</u>.

4) Marco tries to <u>smooth</u> things over — he encourages Eddie to correct Rodolpho when he does something <u>wrong</u>, and <u>instructs</u> Rodolpho to do as Eddie says — "come home early".

Eddie gives Rodolpho a boxing lesson

KEY EVENT

1) Eddie uses a <u>boxing</u> lesson to release his <u>frustrations</u> with Rodolpho.

- At first the others think it's just a bit of <u>fun</u>, but Eddie is taking it more <u>seriously</u> — he wants to show Rodolpho he's <u>stronger</u> than him. Eddie keeps calling Rodolpho "kid" to reinforce his <u>superiority</u>.

- When he hits Rodolpho, Rodolpho *"mildly <u>staggers</u>"* and the others realise that Eddie's <u>crossed a line</u>. Marco *"rises"*, <u>suspicious</u> of Eddie's motives.

- Catherine <u>rushes</u> to Rodolpho when he's hurt. This shows she'll take <u>Rodolpho's side</u> if pushed.

© Donald Cooper/photostage.co.uk

2) After the fight Rodolpho <u>dances</u> with Catherine again — he could be showing Eddie he's <u>not afraid</u> of him.

Marco gives Eddie a warning

KEY EVENT

1) Marco asks Eddie if he can lift a <u>chair</u> from the bottom of one leg, using only one hand. Eddie tries and <u>fails</u> several times. Marco then lifts the chair *"over his head"*, showing that he's <u>stronger</u> than him.

2) This is a <u>warning</u> to Eddie to leave his <u>brother</u> alone — he holds the chair *"like a <u>weapon</u>"* and gives Eddie a *"glare of warning"*. Eddie understands Marco's <u>intention</u> — his *"grin vanishes as he absorbs his [Marco's] look"*.

3) Eddie's domestic <u>authority</u> has been <u>challenged</u> for the first time — he's starting to <u>lose control</u>.

> **Theme — Family**
>
> Marco's reaction shows his <u>loyalty</u> to his brother, and how far he'd go to <u>protect</u> him.

KEY QUOTE

"the chair raised like a weapon over Eddie's head"

Eddie can't lift the chair, and he just *"absorbs"* Marco's look — like a big sponge. Now he knows he'll be taking on both brothers if he tries to get rid of Rodolpho. He should have accepted defeat and given up...

Analysis of Act Two — Eddie Betrays His Family

Now we're onto the second (and final) act of the play, things start to get heated. Catherine and Rodolpho have their first argument and Eddie happens to get home just in time to notice that they've been 'making up'.

Catherine questions Rodolpho's motives

Writer's Techniques

It's never clear what Rodolpho's true motives really are — Miller makes his character deliberately ambiguous.

1) Things are uneasy between Catherine and Rodolpho — Catherine "seems withdrawn" and Rodolpho says she is "full of secrets".

2) Catherine asks Rodolpho if he'd marry her if they had to live in Italy. Rodolpho's response doesn't make his motives any clearer:

Rodolpho says he doesn't want to live in Italy because they'd have to live in poverty — a sensible argument.	BUT	It's the first time he's spoken practically — either he's matured (see p.29) or it isn't the real reason.
He says he wants to marry her and be a citizen — it seems like he's being honest with her.	BUT	He never actually says he loves Catherine — maybe he'd have married any girl who showed an interest.
He is "furious" and offended by Catherine's accusation.	BUT	He could just be angry that Eddie's interfering with the marriage and his chance for citizenship.

Catherine is torn between the two men

1) Catherine says she's "afraid" of Eddie and wants to get away, but she still hopes her relationship with Eddie can go back to how it was before. This shows her naivety — things have already gone too far.

2) Catherine blames Beatrice for Eddie's problems, as she's "goin' at him all the time". She is still blind to Eddie's true feelings.

3) She tells Rodolpho that she loves him and asks him to "Teach" her.

Eddie snaps when he finds them together

1) Eddie arrives while they're in the bedroom. He's "drunk" and a confrontation seems likely.

2) Eddie is furious that they have been intimate together and tells Rodolpho to "get outa here". Catherine wants to leave too, but Eddie wants her to stay. In frustration, he "kisses her on the mouth".

3) Rodolpho attacks Eddie but Eddie easily overpowers him, and then insults him further by kissing him (see p.41). Eddie threatens Rodolpho and tells him to stay away.

© Donald Cooper/photostage.co.uk

Write about how Catherine's decisions affect the plot...

Now that everything's out in the open, Catherine has finally made up her mind. She's chosen Rodolpho over Eddie — show that you understand that this means Eddie is ready to do anything to get rid of his rival.

Analysis of Act Two — Eddie Betrays His Family

This is the moment where Eddie stabs the whole of Red Hook community in the back with a payphone — not an easy task. It'd take absolutely ages. After this scene, there's no going back...

Alfieri warns Eddie to give up

1) Eddie tells Alfieri that his <u>struggle</u> with Rodolpho proves he's <u>gay</u> — "He didn't give me the <u>right</u> kind of <u>fight</u>". Eddie says that he did it to <u>show</u> Catherine "what he [Rodolpho] is".

2) Alfieri says that Rodolpho is "<u>Morally and legally</u>" in the right. The emphasis on "Morally" could show that Alfieri doesn't just think Eddie is wrong in the eyes of the law, but also that he thinks Eddie's feelings are <u>unnatural</u>.

3) He tells Eddie to "<u>Let her go</u>" — he understands Eddie is having difficulty letting Catherine <u>grow up</u>.

Eddie commits the ultimate betrayal

1) The audience realises that Eddie is considering <u>calling</u> the <u>Immigration</u> office as the *"phone booth begins to <u>glow</u>"* at the side of the stage.

2) Alfieri also guesses what Eddie is thinking, and warns him that everyone will "<u>despise</u>" him, and he "won't have a friend in the world". This echoes the story of <u>Vinny Bolzano</u> (see p.11).

© Geraint Lewis / Alamy

3) The *"phone is glowing"* as Eddie picks it up and calls Immigration to <u>report</u> Marco and Rodolpho. This shows the <u>significance</u> of the event.

> **Theme — Honour**
>
> In his desperation, Eddie loses his sense of honour and <u>betrays</u> his family — something he wouldn't normally have <u>dreamt</u> of.

Beatrice and Eddie argue again

1) The cousins have moved upstairs, but the <u>arguments</u> continue between Beatrice and Eddie. Beatrice says she's "sick and tired", but Eddie isn't willing to take any <u>responsibility</u> because she was the one who "brought them" to Red Hook.

2) Eddie sees himself as the <u>victim</u>, saying their house is like a "<u>shootin' gallery</u>" and that he's "<u>the pigeon</u>".

3) Beatrice wants to <u>pretend</u> that nothing has happened and <u>regrets</u> ever letting her cousins stay, <u>wishing</u> she'd dropped dead first.

4) They still <u>argue</u> about what's <u>best</u> for Catherine. Beatrice tells him that she and Rodolpho are getting <u>married</u> next week, and that he should be <u>happy</u> for her.

"Put it out of your mind! Eddie!"

The audience is used to seeing Alfieri as a calm narrator, but even he loses his cool as he realises what Eddie is thinking of doing. Alfieri's reaction makes it clear that Eddie's actions are not going to be taken lightly...

Analysis of Act Two — Eddie Betrays His Family

When Eddie finds out about the other "submarines", his betrayal becomes a whole different kettle of fish — and he'd know all about fish, working on the docks. Eddie realises his betrayal will affect the whole community...

Two new arrivals make Eddie's betrayal more serious

© Photofest

1) Eddie has one last attempt to <u>stop</u> Catherine and Rodolpho's <u>marriage</u>. He says he'd let her "meet some fellas" if she stays, and <u>admits</u> he kept her "home too much". This shows how <u>desperate</u> he's become. It's <u>too little, too late</u> though — Catherine's made up her mind.

2) When Eddie learns two other <u>immigrants</u> are staying with their upstairs neighbours, along with Marco and Rodolpho, he <u>panics</u> — he's worried about how the <u>community</u> will react to his <u>betrayal</u>.

3) However, it's <u>too late</u> for Eddie to do anything about it — shortly afterwards the <u>Immigration</u> authorities arrive to <u>arrest</u> the cousins and the new "submarines".

KEY EVENT

4) Beatrice knows Eddie's responsible <u>straightaway</u>, asking him "My God, what did you do?" She's <u>disgusted</u> and can't believe that he could stoop so <u>low</u>.

Marco publicly accuses Eddie of betrayal

1) As Marco's taken away, he <u>spits</u> in Eddie's face to show his <u>disgust</u>. Eddie <u>threatens</u> to kill Marco and shouts that he "don't forget".

2) Out in the street, Marco <u>points</u> at Eddie and says "I accuse that one!" This public accusation means that Eddie's <u>reputation</u> has been damaged in front of the entire <u>neighbourhood</u>.

3) The locals, including his <u>friends</u> Louis and Mike, <u>turn their backs</u> on Eddie. Eddie continues to <u>protest</u> his <u>innocence</u>, <u>threatening</u> to kill Marco over and over.

Theme — Honour

Eddie is <u>furious</u> that he has been humiliated in <u>public</u> — but it was his <u>dishonourable betrayal</u> of Marco and Rodolpho that caused Marco to <u>spit</u> at him.

Marco promises not to harm Eddie

Bail is when a prisoner is temporarily released from prison while they await their trial.

1) Alfieri tries to secure <u>bail</u> for Marco and Rodolpho before their hearings come up, but he needs Marco to <u>agree</u> not to <u>harm</u> Eddie if he is released. Marco says that in Italy Eddie "would be dead now", showing how <u>seriously</u> Italians take this kind of <u>betrayal</u>.

2) Alfieri understands that there's <u>legal</u> justice (the law) and <u>moral</u> justice (God's justice), but Marco <u>refuses</u> to put faith in either — he says "All the law is not in a book" and would rather take his <u>own</u> justice than wait for God.

3) When Marco eventually agrees, it "*seems he is <u>ashamed</u>*" — he's betraying his own <u>principles</u> by saying he will not harm Eddie. It also <u>hints</u> to the audience that Marco is unlikely to <u>keep</u> his promise.

Theme — Justice

Marco wants justice, and if the <u>law</u> can't give it to him, Eddie will have to be punished in <u>another way</u>.

EXAM TIP

Mention how Miller builds tension...

You could, for example, discuss how Miller builds tension by having Marco accuse Eddie publicly. This creates tension because the audience knows that Eddie will have to confront Marco to save his reputation.

Analysis of Act Two — Eddie Betrays His Family

So, here it is, the glittering finale of *A View from the Bridge*. We all knew it would end in tragedy for Eddie, one way or another. Nobody really gets a happy ending — it's just another gritty fairy tale of New York.

Eddie's family has fallen apart

1) The scene opens with Eddie "*alone in the rocker*". This symbolises how Eddie has been <u>isolated</u> by his actions.

2) Eddie tells Beatrice that if she goes to the <u>wedding</u> she "ain't comin' back". Eddie wants "<u>respect</u>", and won't let Beatrice go unless Marco <u>apologises</u> — he's still playing the <u>victim</u>.

3) Catherine is <u>furious</u> — she says Eddie's "a <u>rat</u>" who has no "right to tell nobody nothin'!" Despite everything, Beatrice still <u>defends</u> him.

4) Beatrice tries to make <u>peace</u> by agreeing to <u>stay</u> with Eddie. She also urges Eddie to <u>accept</u> Rodolpho's <u>apology</u> and warns him not to <u>confront</u> Marco.

5) Before Marco arrives, Beatrice is so <u>desperate</u> to avoid violence that she confronts Eddie about his <u>unnatural feelings</u> for Catherine. Eddie claims he just wants his "<u>name</u>" but Beatrice says he wants "somethin' else... and you can never have her!" She thinks that "The <u>truth</u> is not as bad as <u>blood</u>".

Marco confronts Eddie

When Marco calls Eddie outside, Eddie <u>welcomes</u> the opportunity to save his <u>reputation</u>:

- He <u>repeats</u> his own name over and over, as if trying to get back his <u>ruined</u> reputation.
- He says that if Marco <u>apologises</u> they can go to the wedding together — this obviously won't work as it was the <u>marriage</u> he had the issue with in the first place.

Eddie is killed with his own knife

Eddie is killed by his own blade. This symbolises that he's responsible for his own downfall (see p.50).

KEY EVENT

1) Marco <u>attacks</u> Eddie, and Eddie tries to <u>stab</u> him. However, Marco grabs Eddie's arm and turns the knife towards Eddie who is <u>stabbed</u>.

2) As Eddie dies, Catherine screams that she never <u>meant</u> to "do nothing bad" to him. He begins to ask "Then why —". He still can't take <u>responsibility</u> for what's happened. Eddie calls for <u>Beatrice</u> — the only person still on his <u>side</u>.

3) Alfieri <u>concludes</u> the play by telling the audience that he knew "how wrong" Eddie was, and that his death was "<u>useless</u>". However, he still <u>mourns</u> and <u>admires</u> Eddie for being "wholly known" — he showed everyone his <u>true self</u>.

Theme — Conflict

It's only in her <u>final</u> words that Catherine becomes fully <u>aware</u> of how she has affected Eddie and that she's partly <u>responsible</u> for the play's main <u>conflict</u>.

KEY QUOTE

"I think I will love him more than all my sensible clients."

At the end of the play, Eddie's lost pretty much everything, including his life. Alfieri still loves him, though, because he was always true to himself — bless. So there is a silver lining, although it's a very fine one...

Practice Questions

So now you've had the chance to look at the play in more detail, everything should be becoming nice and clear to you. See how much you remember about Act One by giving these quick questions a go.

Quick Questions — Act One

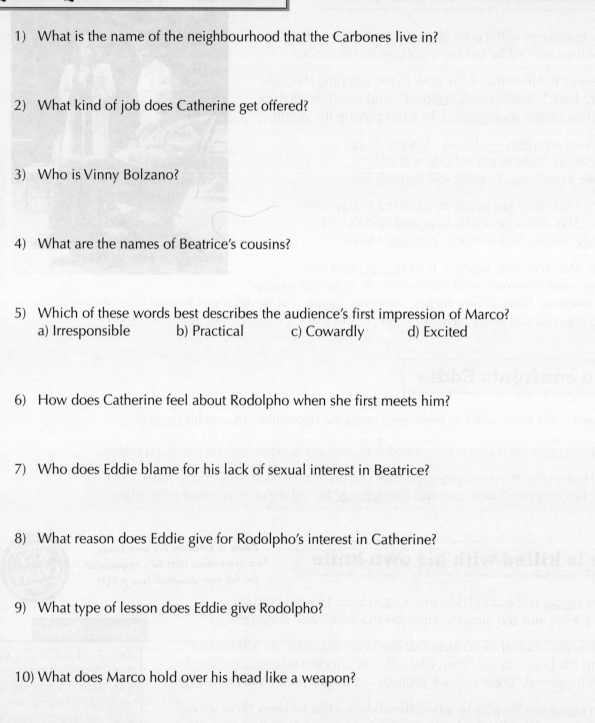

1) What is the name of the neighbourhood that the Carbones live in?

2) What kind of job does Catherine get offered?

3) Who is Vinny Bolzano?

4) What are the names of Beatrice's cousins?

5) Which of these words best describes the audience's first impression of Marco?
   a) Irresponsible   b) Practical   c) Cowardly   d) Excited

6) How does Catherine feel about Rodolpho when she first meets him?

7) Who does Eddie blame for his lack of sexual interest in Beatrice?

8) What reason does Eddie give for Rodolpho's interest in Catherine?

9) What type of lesson does Eddie give Rodolpho?

10) What does Marco hold over his head like a weapon?

Practice Questions

Hopefully, those questions weren't too tricky — you can always have another look over the section if there are any bits you can't quite remember. This page is more of the same — but about Act Two.

Quick Questions — Act Two

1) What is Rodolpho's reason for not wanting to live in Italy?

2) What event makes Eddie throw Rodolpho out of the house?

3) Who does Eddie try to convince that Rodolpho is gay?

4) What causes Eddie to panic before the Immigration officers arrive?

5) Where does Marco accuse Eddie of betraying him?

6) Find two quotes from Act Two that show that Eddie thinks he's a victim.

7) Why do Louis and Mike turn their backs on Eddie?

8) What promise must Marco make before he can be given bail?

9) Where does Eddie stop Beatrice from going?

10) How does Eddie die?

Practice Questions

You only need to write a few lines for each of the in-depth questions, but try to refer to the play as much as possible. The exam-style questions are more or less what you'd expect to see in the exam. Give a couple a go, then take a tea-break and dream about the results-day glory that all your hard work will earn you.

In-depth Questions

1) Why do you think Miller included the story about Vinny Bolzano?

2) Do you think that Rodolpho really loves Catherine? Why?

3) Do you think Beatrice mainly has selfish motives when she warns Catherine about her behaviour? Explain your answer.

4) Why do you think Marco warns Eddie by lifting a chair above his head instead of telling him directly?

5) Why do you think Eddie continues to act like the victim, even though he's guilty of calling the Immigration department?

Exam-style Questions

1) Read the passage that begins "ALFIERI: You wouldn't have known it" (the beginning of Act One) and ends with "run its bloody course". How effective is Alfieri's speech as an introduction to the play's setting and the events that will unfold during the play?

2) How does Miller show that Catherine has matured over the course of the play?

3) "You can quicker get back a million dollars... than a word that you gave away". To what extent do you think this line sums up the play's message?

4) How does Miller use the conversation between Eddie and Alfieri in Act One to represent the wider issues and concerns of the play as a whole?

Character Profile — Alfieri

Alfieri is the narrator of the story, who predicts that all will end in tragedy. As a lawyer, he tries to advise the other characters, but all he can do is make suggestions — that doesn't mean they'll actually listen...

Alfieri is a lawyer in Red Hook

Alfieri's background means he can act as a 'bridge' between the American and Italian communities (see p.50).

1) Alfieri is a *"portly"* lawyer *"in his fifties"*. He's also the narrator who sets up the story for the audience.

2) Alfieri grew up in Italy, so he can empathise with "the petty troubles of the poor".

3) He helps the audience understand why the law isn't a "friendly idea" for most Italians — in Italy it is associated with trouble, not justice.

4) He explains the difference between what is *"legal"* and what people feel is right — the law can't always give people the justice they want.

Alfieri is...

wise: "I knew where he was going to end"

powerless: "I was so powerless to stop it"

moral: "To promise not to kill is not dishonourable"

© Donald Cooper/photostage.co.uk

He prepares the audience for what's going to happen

1) As the narrator, Alfieri speaks with hindsight — the play's events have already happened so he knows how it will end.

2) Alfieri warns the audience there will be a tragic ending right from the start when he says lawyers are "thought of in connection with disasters" and that the play will "run its bloody course".

3) He also hints at the play's ending in his first meeting with Eddie. He warns that Eddie has "too much love for the niece" and says that, even without hindsight, he could see "every step coming".

Alfieri is powerless to prevent tragedy

1) Eddie and Marco's actions are fuelled by their feelings and sense of honour. This means that Alfieri is unable to reason with them.

2) Both Eddie and Marco ask Alfieri to do something about what has happened, but the law has not been broken, so he is powerless. Alfieri believes that "Only God makes justice".

3) Even though Alfieri could see what was happening, he couldn't sound the "alarm" or call the police because "nothing [had] happened". Like the audience, he can only watch the events unfold.

Writer's Techniques

Alfieri is the only character who speaks in Standard English. This shows that he is well-educated and that he represents American law, rather than the unwritten law of the Italian immigrants.

KEY QUOTE

"I could see every step coming, step after step"

Alfieri may have had a feeling about what might happen, but he couldn't stop it. He's like a weatherman — he'd be more useful if he could prevent bad things, rather than just telling us there's a storm coming...

Character Profile — Eddie

Eddie's a bit of a mixed-up character — he's not all good or bad. He's a hard-working man with family values. But some of those values go out of the window when his feelings and desires get the better of him.

Eddie is a hard-working family man

Longshoremen are dockworkers who load and unload the ships.

1) Eddie is the <u>main character</u> in the play. He's about *"forty — a husky, slightly overweight <u>longshoreman</u>"*.

2) He took in his <u>niece</u>, Catherine, as if she was his own child, showing he's <u>generous</u> and <u>compassionate</u>.

3) He's <u>respected</u> by his friends and family. Mike says he's "got a lotta credit" coming to him for <u>taking in</u> immigrants, and Beatrice says he'll "get a <u>blessing</u>".

4) However, his <u>jealousy</u> makes him act out of <u>character</u> when he reports the cousins to Immigration.

> **Eddie is...**
>
> **hard-working:** "I worked like a dog twenty years"
> **generous:** "we got plenty of room"
> **controlling:** "you can't be so friendly, kid"
> **jealous:** "you're just jealous"

Eddie and Beatrice have a complex relationship

1) At the <u>beginning</u> of the play, Eddie and Beatrice have an <u>affectionate</u> relationship:

- Eddie shows genuine <u>concern</u> for Beatrice, and doesn't want her cousins to take <u>advantage</u> of her — "she's got too big a heart".

- He also <u>respects</u> her <u>opinions</u>, and lets Catherine go to work when Beatrice <u>pleads</u> with him.

- Beatrice <u>dotes</u> on Eddie, calling him an "<u>angel</u>" and holding his <u>face</u> in her <u>hands</u>. Eddie enjoys this, <u>smiling</u> gratefully.

2) But as the play goes on it's clear that there are <u>cracks</u> in their marriage:

- When Eddie realises Catherine will soon <u>leave</u> home, and Beatrice tries to comfort him, he *"turns his head away"*, <u>rejecting</u> her affection.

- It's clear that their relationship has not been <u>sexual</u> for months when Beatrice asks, "When am I gonna be a wife again, Eddie?"

© Donald Cooper/photostage.co.uk

Eddie and Catherine are very close

1) Eddie <u>dotes</u> on his niece and only wants the <u>best</u> for her — he wants her to have a good job and "to be with <u>different</u> kind of people".

2) But he has trouble <u>letting her go</u> — he wants her to <u>stay</u> <u>with him</u> — child or not — for as long as possible.

3) However, both Beatrice and Alfieri realise that Eddie's <u>love</u> for Catherine has become more than <u>fatherly</u> — "there is too much love for the niece".

4) Eddie goes from seeing her as a "<u>baby</u>" to comparing her to "Garbo" — an actress who was famed for being glamorous. This <u>fantasy</u> image shows that his love for Catherine has become <u>unnatural</u>.

> **Theme — Family**
>
> Eddie is a <u>father figure</u> to Catherine. However, as his <u>role</u> in her life becomes unclear, his relationship as a <u>husband</u> to Beatrice also <u>weakens</u>.

Character Profile — Eddie

Eddie is also quite the control-freak — keeping tabs on everyone and everything in his household. Maybe that's why he acts like such a madman when he can't control his own feelings.

He likes to be in control...

Eddie wants to be in control of his household and he's always telling Beatrice and Catherine what to do:

- He tries to stop Catherine from wearing certain clothes, working and from having relationships.

- He even tries to control what Beatrice thinks, telling her that "A wife is supposed to believe the husband".

- He stops Beatrice from going to the wedding by giving her an ultimatum — "You walk out that door... you ain't comin' back".

Theme — Men & Women

Eddie believes that men should be manly and in charge of the household. Having the "respect" of his family is important to him.

...but he can't control his feelings

1) He often gets teary-eyed when he realises that Catherine is growing up.

2) He takes a disliking to Rodolpho straightaway because Catherine is attracted to him. Eddie's hatred of Rodolpho is clear when Catherine and Rodolpho dance. He "unconsciously" twists a newspaper "into a tight roll", making it weapon-like — he can't control his anger.

3) By the end of the play Eddie can't even control his feelings in public, shouting "I'll kill him! I'll kill him!" as Marco is taken away.

Theme — Honour

Honour is very important to the men in the play. Eddie only acts dishonourably when he loses control of his feelings — his jealousy makes him act irrationally.

His unnatural love for Catherine leads to his downfall

1) Eddie acts rashly because he is ruled by his desires and emotions — his jealousy of Rodolpho leads him to break his code of honour and betray the cousins.

2) This means he loses his respect and his good "name", which are so important to him.

3) But, Eddie doesn't lose Beatrice's love — he dies in her arms and his last words are, "My B.!"

4) Alfieri still loves him too — he admires him for having allowed himself to be "wholly known".

5) Eddie is in "a strange sort of relaxation" before his fight with Marco — he may have seen death as an honourable way out of a dishonoured existence.

© Donald Cooper/photostage.co.uk

EXAM TIP

Discuss how Miller presents Eddie as a complex character...

It's tempting to only focus on Eddie's flaws, but keep in mind that Miller makes him a sympathetic character. He's shown to be generous, compassionate and loved by his family — this makes his downfall more tragic.

Character Profile — Beatrice

Beatrice is stuck in the middle of this whole drama — and not just in a literal sense. She's selfless and tries to keep everyone happy — she's the glue that holds them all together. She's just not quite sticky enough...

Beatrice wants a happy family life

1) Beatrice is Eddie's <u>wife</u>, Catherine's <u>aunt</u>, and Marco and Rodolpho's <u>cousin</u>.

2) Although Eddie accuses her of having "never worked", she works pretty <u>hard</u> at home and is always doing some sort of <u>household chore</u> for the family.

3) She spends most of her time looking after <u>others</u> and trying to keep <u>everyone happy</u>. She tries to <u>help</u> both Eddie and Catherine when she realises that his <u>feelings</u> for Catherine have become <u>more</u> than fatherly.

Beatrice is...

caring: "she's got too big a heart"

loyal: "Whatever happened we all done it"

perceptive: "The truth is not as bad as blood"

Beatrice is a loyal and loving wife...

1) Beatrice puts up with a <u>lot</u> for Eddie:

- His lack of <u>sexual</u> interest — she worries that it's her fault: "am I doing something wrong?"

- His <u>inappropriate</u> feelings towards her niece — she tries to <u>help</u> even though it's <u>upsetting</u> for her.

2) But she still <u>loves</u> Eddie and <u>defends</u> him until the end:

- When Catherine calls Eddie a "rat", Beatrice is <u>furious</u>. She shouts, "Don't you call him that!"

- Even when she <u>confronts</u> him about his unnatural feelings, she's on <u>his side</u>: "Listen... I love you".

- She is unable to <u>abandon</u> Eddie to go to Catherine's <u>wedding</u>, even though she <u>wants</u> to go.

...and a caring aunt

1) Beatrice <u>supports</u> Catherine when she wants to start <u>working</u>, telling Eddie, "she's gotta go to work sometime".

2) She also gives Catherine <u>advice</u>, helping her to become her <u>own person</u> and make her <u>own decisions</u>.

3) She <u>genuinely</u> wants Catherine to be happy — she isn't just trying to get her out of the house. She still loves Catherine like a <u>daughter</u> even though Catherine has accidentally caused <u>problems</u> in her marriage.

Theme — Family

Family is extremely <u>important</u> to Beatrice. As well as trying to give Catherine the best <u>start in life</u>, she does <u>all she can</u> for Marco and Rodolpho, who she'd never even met before.

Character Profile — Beatrice

Beatrice is pretty clued-up when it comes to understanding people. She knows Eddie better than anyone and can see that he's gotten a bit too fond of Catherine before he even realises it himself.

Beatrice is very perceptive

© Elliott Franks / ArenaPAL

1) Beatrice <u>understands</u> that a "grown woman" like Catherine, living "with a grown man" has to "<u>act different</u>". She tells Catherine that if she acts like a baby, Eddie will "be treatin' you like a baby".

2) She realises that Eddie's <u>behaviour</u> towards Catherine has become <u>inappropriate</u> and warns him that he needs to "be an <u>uncle</u>"— not a <u>father</u> or a <u>lover</u>.

3) She <u>realises</u> that Eddie is responsible for calling Immigration <u>straightaway</u>, despite his denials.

4) Beatrice also <u>foresees</u> that things will end in <u>tragedy</u> unless Eddie resolves his <u>conflict</u> with the cousins.

She always puts others before herself

1) Eddie recalls that they had to <u>sleep</u> on the <u>floor</u> for two weeks when Beatrice's <u>parents</u> came to stay.

2) She <u>confronts</u> Eddie about letting Catherine work, saying that she's "crazy to start", even though she's <u>afraid</u> of how he will react.

3) Beatrice is <u>tactful</u> when she explains to Catherine that her behaviour could make a wife <u>jealous</u> — she doesn't want to <u>hurt</u> her.

4) After her cousins have moved out, Beatrice feels so <u>guilty</u> that she wishes she was "dead", even though it's not her <u>fault</u>.

> **Theme — Men & Women**
>
> Beatrice is meant to be a <u>stereotypical 1950s</u> woman — a <u>loyal</u> housewife who stays at home and <u>cares</u> for the family.

She tries to prevent and resolve conflicts

1) Even before her <u>cousins</u> arrive Beatrice tries to avoid potential conflict by offering to "tell them to go <u>someplace else</u>".

2) She tries to <u>prevent</u> Eddie opposing Catherine getting a <u>job</u> by suggesting he "eat first" to put him in a good <u>mood</u>.

3) At the end of the play she wants Eddie to <u>make up</u> with Rodolpho to help <u>pacify</u> Marco, and tries to avoid <u>bloodshed</u> by confronting Eddie with the <u>truth</u> — "You want somethin' else, Eddie, and you can <u>never have her</u>!"

> **Theme — Conflict**
>
> Even when Beatrice does <u>initiate</u> a <u>conflict</u>, e.g. confronting Eddie about letting Catherine <u>work</u>, she does it to <u>prevent</u> further conflict in the <u>long run</u> — if Eddie lets Catherine go, there'd be no more conflict in their <u>marriage</u>.

KEY QUOTE

"go to your wedding, Katie, I'll stay home."

Poor B — she wants to go to Catherine's wedding, but she decides to stay home to keep Eddie happy. I always say that being nice gets you nowhere — you wouldn't believe what I had to do to get this job...

Character Profile — Catherine

Catherine is Beatrice's niece and she's been raised by the Carbones since she was a baby. She loves them as if they were her parents, and is blissfully unaware that she's the source of the couple's troubles.

Catherine is the Carbones' beautiful and much-loved niece

1) Catherine is <u>seventeen</u>. According to Eddie she is so <u>beautiful</u> that she turns heads "like windmills".

2) Eddie and Beatrice brought Catherine up as their own daughter after her mother's <u>death</u>. Catherine <u>relies</u> on them for support.

3) By <u>Red Hook</u> standards, she's <u>well-educated</u> — she is training as a <u>stenographer</u> and has just been offered a <u>job</u>.

4) She falls in <u>love</u> with Rodolpho, and spends the rest of the play trying to get Eddie's <u>approval</u> for their relationship.

Catherine is...
naive: "I don't know anything"
childlike: "*you* think you're a baby"
emotional: "*She is at the edge of tears*"
passionate: "Who the hell do you think you are?"

A stenographer is a kind of assistant who makes notes and takes dictations.

She and Eddie have an intense relationship

1) Eddie is Catherine's <u>father figure</u> — at the start of the play she seeks his <u>approval</u> for everything, and whenever he <u>disapproves</u> she's "*almost in <u>tears</u>*".

2) She still acts like a <u>child</u> around him — <u>throwing</u> herself at him like she "was twelve years old". This makes Eddie treat her like a <u>baby</u>.

3) She <u>resents</u> how <u>controlling</u> he can be — she is "*<u>Embarrassed</u>*" and "*<u>angered</u>*" when Eddie makes her change out of her <u>high-heels</u>.

4) She finds it hard to <u>reject</u> him — "You think it's so easy to... say to a man he's nothin' to you". She's <u>torn</u> between the two men in her life.

© Geraint Lewis / Alamy

Catherine is a foil to Beatrice

A foil is a character who shares similarities, but also some important differences, with another character. This emphasises each character's key characteristics.

1) Throughout the play, Catherine acts as a <u>foil</u> to Beatrice:

Catherine is...
- <u>Young</u> — she's got her whole life <u>ahead</u> of her.
- <u>Naive</u> — she doesn't know how the <u>world</u> works.
- <u>Becoming independent</u> — she wants a <u>job</u> to make money, so she can <u>move out</u>.

Beatrice is...
- <u>Middle-aged</u> — her life is unlikely to <u>change</u>.
- <u>Worldly</u> — she's <u>experienced</u> enough to recognise when things are going <u>wrong</u>.
- <u>Dependent</u> — she <u>relies</u> on Eddie for everything.

2) Catherine's <u>relationship</u> with Rodolpho also <u>contrasts</u> with Beatrice's relationship with Eddie:

Catherine and Rodolpho's relationship
- They both seem to be <u>happy</u> and in <u>love</u> with each other. They <u>rarely</u> seem to argue.
- Catherine <u>criticises</u> Beatrice for <u>neglecting</u> Eddie's needs. She thinks she'd make a better <u>wife</u>.

Eddie and Beatrice's relationship
- They are <u>unhappy</u> — they argue a <u>lot</u> and haven't got on for months.
- But <u>Beatrice</u> also has <u>needs</u>, and she actually always puts Eddie before herself.

Character Profile — Catherine

Catherine matures a lot during the play — she stops whining and starts to take action. She learns to make her own decisions as she gets ready to fly the nest. To be honest, I'd fly away too — the Carbones are crayzee...

Catherine is instantly attracted to Rodolpho

© Tristram Kenton/Lebrecht Music & Arts

1) As soon as Catherine sees Rodolpho she is <u>struck</u> by the fact he's "a real <u>blond</u>", and is "*enthralled*" by his <u>singing</u>.

2) She doesn't <u>hide</u> her <u>interest</u> in Rodolpho, almost <u>immediately</u> asking, "You married too?" She's <u>open</u>, uncalculating and she's <u>naive</u> about relationships.

3) She falls so in <u>love</u> with Rodolpho that she doesn't want to believe that he might have more <u>sinister motives</u>, even though they're a bit <u>unclear</u> (see p.29).

> **Theme — Love**
>
> Catherine is <u>torn</u> between her <u>daughterly</u> love for Eddie and her <u>romantic</u> love for Rodolpho.

Catherine's naivety is her greatest weakness

1) Catherine's <u>naivety</u> makes her behave <u>inappropriately</u> with Eddie — walking around the apartment in only her <u>slip</u>.

> **Theme — Men & Women**
>
> It's <u>ironic</u> when Catherine asks "why don't she [Beatrice] be a <u>woman</u>?" when she doesn't <u>understand</u> how to be a woman <u>herself</u>. She thinks being a woman means being able to make a <u>man happy</u>.

2) Beatrice has to explain to Catherine how things really are — she's <u>growing up</u>, and she has to <u>change</u> how she acts.

3) Catherine doesn't <u>realise</u> that she's caused <u>problems</u> for Eddie and Beatrice. Beatrice <u>laughs sadly</u> at the fact that Catherine has never considered that Beatrice might be <u>jealous</u> of her.

4) Rodolpho also tells her that she needs to grow up — comparing her to a "little <u>bird</u>", and telling her it is <u>time</u> "to <u>fly</u>". Eventually, she begs Rodolpho to "<u>teach</u>" her how to be a <u>woman</u>.

By the end of the play she is more assertive

1) Deciding to marry Rodolpho is a real <u>turning point</u> for Catherine — she <u>tells</u> Eddie she's "not gonna be a <u>baby</u> any more!"

2) When Eddie forces a <u>kiss</u> on her, she tries to take <u>control</u> of the situation for the first time, telling Rodolpho to "Wait outside" while she deals with Eddie.

3) Her new found <u>assertiveness</u> is expressed verbally when she says Eddie belongs in the "garbage", and even <u>physically</u> when she "*tears at Eddie's face*" to stop him kissing Rodolpho.

KEY QUOTE

"I'm not gonna be a baby any more!"

Catherine ages like a Stilton — she gets stronger, more mature and... smellier? Not quite, but she does change a lot in the play. You might say she goes straight from being a baby to getting married — bizarre...

Character Profile — Rodolpho

At the start of the play, Rodolpho is a happy-go-lucky day-dreamer with no real responsibilities. He's young and still has a positive outlook on the world — I'm not so sure he feels the same way by the end though...

Rodolpho is young, carefree and single

1) Rodolpho is Beatrice's <u>cousin</u> and Marco's <u>younger</u> brother. He has come to America for <u>work</u>, but hopes to <u>stay</u> for good.

2) As well as having "a nice face" and unusually <u>fair</u> hair for an <u>Italian</u>, Rodolpho can <u>sing</u>, make <u>clothes</u> and is a "very good <u>cook</u>".

3) Rodolpho doesn't <u>notice</u> Eddie's <u>hostility</u> at first — he's too busy laughing and <u>enjoying</u> himself.

4) He makes <u>light</u> of <u>sad</u> things, like the fact that the horses in his home town are "skinnier than <u>goats</u>".

> **Rodolpho is...**
>
> **skilled:** "He sings, he cooks, he could make dresses"
> **attractive:** "He's a real blond!"
> **light-hearted:** "In our town the horses are only for show"

He looks up to his older brother

1) Marco and Rodolpho are very <u>close</u> and seem to have spent a lot of time together in <u>Italy</u> — they <u>worked together</u> and <u>shared</u> the profits: "Marco is a mason and I bring the cement".

2) Before <u>singing</u> "Paper Doll" for Catherine, he waits for a "*nod of <u>permission</u>*" from Marco. Then, when Marco <u>tells</u> him to "be quiet", he just <u>nods</u>. The fact that the brothers can <u>communicate</u> without speaking suggests that they are very <u>close</u>.

3) Rodolpho does what Marco <u>says</u> throughout the play — he agrees to "<u>come home early</u>" when Marco asks him to.

> **Theme — Sexuality**
>
> Rodolpho's <u>talents</u> make the other dockers think that he's not <u>masculine</u> enough. Eddie thinks he's gay, but there's no real <u>evidence</u> for this (see p.40).

He wants to make Catherine happy

1) Catherine is part of Rodolpho's <u>American dream</u> — he dreams of going to <u>Broadway</u> "with her" to see the theatres and the opera.

The American Dream was the idea that America was a place where anyone could achieve anything, regardless of their background.

2) He seems to <u>genuinely care</u> for Catherine, she says that he "almost bows" to her, and takes her <u>arm</u> when they walk in the street.

3) He is <u>sensitive</u> to her moods and <u>notices</u> when she is upset, asking, "What worries you, Catherine?" He's <u>perceptive</u> enough to realise that <u>Eddie</u> is behind Catherine's <u>worries</u>.

4) By discussing their problems, their <u>relationship</u> becomes a good <u>foil</u> to the relationship between <u>Beatrice and Eddie</u>, whose <u>communication</u> is <u>terrible</u>.

See p.26 for more on foils.

Character Profile — Rodolpho

Rodolpho is like a kid in a sweet shop, enjoying the exciting new experiences that America has to offer. He can make a joke out of even the most depressing subjects — a man after my own heart.

Rodolpho is passionate about life in America

1) Rodolpho is "crazy for New York", and all things American — the movies, jazz, and the bright lights.

2) Rodolpho seems materialistic and shallow because he spends his pay on clothes and records, while Marco's children are starving. This could suggest that family loyalty is not that important to him, but he could just be excited to have money to spend for the first time in his life.

Theme — Justice

Rodolpho is more willing to accept the American justice system — he seems to encourage Marco "to settle for half". This suggests that Rodolpho is also happy to turn his back on the Sicilian code (see p.7).

He could just be using Catherine to get citizenship

1) Even though it seems like he loves Catherine, Miller never makes it clear whether or not Rodolpho just wants citizenship.

2) When Catherine asks him if he'd marry her if they had to move to Italy, Rodolpho gets angry and says he wants "to be a citizen".

3) His refusal to consider living in Italy might be because he doesn't want Catherine to "suffer in a poor country", or it might hint at his true motives.

4) Rodolpho does seem genuinely insulted and angry at the suggestion that he would marry someone he didn't love "just to be an American".

5) He says that his "heart dies" when he looks at Catherine — it sounds like he's in love, but he never actually says that he loves her.

© Donald Cooper/photostage.cc.uk

He matures throughout the play

At the start of the play Rodolpho spends his money on records and clothes... **BUT** ... by the end of the play he has saved "nearly three hundred dollars" — he's planning for his future with Catherine.

He starts off light-hearted and can't take anything seriously... **BUT** ... he proves he's matured when he apologises to Eddie — "I have made all our troubles" — even though it's not his fault.

He's submissive at the start of the play, and looks to Marco for how to act... **BUT** ... by the end of the play he's advising Marco what to do: "Marco — promise the man".

Don't forget to talk about the American Dream...

In the exam, Rodolpho is a good character to link to the American Dream — because of Catherine, he gets to start a new life in America. It all seems a bit hollow in the light of everything else that happens, though.

Character Profile — Marco

Marco isn't the most chatty person, but he watches everything closely. Then, when he sees something he doesn't like he turns green and he — let's just say, you wouldn't like him when he's angry.

Marco is the strong, silent type

1) Marco is Rodolpho's older brother and Beatrice's cousin. He's also a husband, and a father to three young children in Italy.

2) He's "a square-built peasant of thirty-two". Unlike Rodolpho, he's admired by Eddie and the other dockworkers:

> • Eddie tells Beatrice that "nobody kids Marco" because he acts like a man.
>
> • Mike describes him as a "regular bull" who could "load the whole ship by himself".

3) Despite his 'macho' appearance he is "tender, and quiet-voiced" — he's a man of few words who never says more than he needs to.

© Donald Cooper/photostage.co.uk

Marco is...

strong: "he's a regular bull"
protective: "He degraded my brother"
honourable: "such a promise is dishonorable"

He feels responsible for Rodolpho

1) In the beginning, Marco speaks on behalf of Rodolpho. When Catherine offers them soup, he declines for them both, without asking Rodolpho if he's hungry.

2) He makes sure Rodolpho behaves correctly, and tells him what to do — "You come home early now".

3) He tries to ground Rodolpho in reality. When Rodolpho talks about living for six months on his singing, Marco corrects him: "Two months". Marco thinks Rodolpho's ideas are just "dreams".

4) When Eddie hits Rodolpho, Marco is quick to protect him. Marco raises a chair above his head "like a weapon" as a warning to Eddie not to hurt his brother.

5) At the end of the play, Marco is comforted by the knowledge that Rodolpho will be able to stay in America, saying, "Well — we did something".

He worries about his wife and children

1) Marco's young children are starving, and one has tuberculosis. When he learns that he will be able to send money back to Italy straightaway he is so relieved that he is "near tears".

2) He really misses his wife — he "smiles shyly" and blushes when he talks about her. He says that she is "very lonesome" without him.

3) When he is arrested, Marco's first thought is his family, shouting "He killed my children". His usual calmness is replaced with angry passion.

Theme — Family

Marco is mainly concerned with his family — he came to America to provide for his children, and is wary of Eddie because he dislikes Rodolpho.

Character Profile — Marco

Marco's sense of honour is what people admire about him — even Eddie. This code of honour stuff seems like a bit of a burden to me though — it just gets you into even more trouble.

Marco is a good house guest

1) Marco doesn't want to <u>outstay</u> his <u>welcome</u>, he says to Eddie "when you say go, we will go".

2) He <u>respects</u> Eddie as <u>head</u> of the house, and tries to <u>smooth</u> things out between Eddie and Rodolpho, asking Eddie to <u>explain</u> how Rodolpho has upset him.

3) When Marco realises that Eddie has <u>hurt</u> Rodolpho, Marco <u>warns</u> him by lifting a <u>chair</u> above his head, rather than resort to physical <u>violence</u> himself. He doesn't want things to <u>escalate</u> any further.

© Donald Cooper/photostage.co.uk

Marco is a foil to Eddie

See p.26 for more on foils.

1) They are both <u>hard-working, responsible family men</u> with a deep sense of <u>honour</u>.

2) However, whilst Eddie's <u>obsession</u> with Catherine completely <u>distorts</u> his personality, Marco <u>stays true</u> to who he is throughout the play.

3) The <u>conflict</u> between the two characters at the play's end is about <u>honour</u>:

- Marco's honour has been <u>offended</u> by Eddie's actions.
- Eddie falsely <u>claims</u> that his honour has been ruined by Marco — it's actually Eddie's <u>own fault</u> that his reputation is in tatters.
- When the two <u>clash</u>, Marco is fighting for <u>true honour</u> whilst Eddie is fighting for <u>false honour</u>.

Theme — Honour

Eddie would probably have also sought <u>revenge</u> in Marco's <u>position</u> — honour is <u>important</u> to them both. In Act One, Eddie seems to agree with <u>violence</u> against an <u>informer</u> (Vinny Bolzano).

Marco believes in the ancient Sicilian code of honour

1) The <u>Sicilian code</u> was the idea that you always dealt with your <u>own</u> problems, and you <u>never</u> involved the <u>authorities</u> (e.g. the <u>police</u> and the <u>government</u>).

2) Marco can't believe that there is no <u>law</u> against what Eddie did. He believes Eddie "<u>degraded</u>" his brother and "<u>robbed</u>" his children, and that it is his <u>duty</u> to <u>avenge</u> the wrongs done to his family.

3) He also believes that "to promise not to kill" under the circumstances would be "<u>dishonorable</u>" — in his country Eddie "<u>would be dead</u> now".

4) It's <u>uncertain</u> if Marco would have <u>killed</u> Eddie if Eddie hadn't taken out a <u>knife</u>, so we'll never know if Marco meant to <u>break</u> his promise to Alfieri. What is clear is that Marco shows no <u>remorse</u> for Eddie's death — he thinks he's <u>morally</u> in the right.

KEY QUOTE *"He degraded my brother. My blood."*

Marco is caught up in a conflict that's really between Eddie and Rodolpho, but his strong sense of honour pushes him to take revenge. He's just another victim of the mess caused by Eddie's feelings for Catherine.

Character Profile — Other Characters

There are a few other characters who aren't that important to the main plot, but who help to put it in context. They represent the community of Red Hook — so it's worth taking note of some of the things they say.

Louis and Mike are typical dockers

1) They are the <u>first</u> characters on stage and they represent the <u>community</u> of <u>Red Hook</u>.

2) They help show some of Eddie's key <u>qualities</u>:

When they <u>make fun</u> of Rodolpho, Eddie <u>defends</u> him, even though he's already in <u>conflict</u> with him: "he's a kid yet, y'know". 	This shows that Eddie thinks that his <u>family's</u> <u>honour</u> is <u>important</u>.
They think that Eddie has "got a <u>lotta credit</u> comin'" to him for helping Beatrice's cousins.	This shows that the community recognises Eddie's <u>generosity</u>.
They provide a <u>foil</u> to Eddie's <u>intensity</u> as they seem quite <u>carefree</u> — they are first seen "*pitching coins*" against a wall, and often go bowling after work.	Meanwhile Eddie is <u>only concerned</u> with his <u>family's well-being</u>, and never seems to have time to go bowling.

© iStockphoto.com/Kevin Russ

3) Mike is also important in <u>fuelling</u> Eddie's fears about Rodolpho's sexuality — he says that everyone at work <u>laughs</u> at Rodolpho because of the strange <u>comments</u> he makes.

4) When they <u>turn</u> their backs on Eddie because of his <u>betrayal</u>, they represent the feelings of the <u>whole</u> community. If Eddie's <u>friends</u> won't side with him, <u>nobody</u> will.

Other Italians are accidentally involved

1) Even though we never see her on stage, <u>Mrs Dondero</u> takes in Marco and Rodolpho and two other <u>immigrants</u>. This shows that there are other <u>generous</u> people living in the community who feel that it's an <u>honour</u> to help immigrants.

2) The Liparis also get involved when Eddie <u>accidentally</u> betrays the Liparis' nephew when he reports the cousins to <u>Immigration</u>.

3) This shows how <u>tangled</u> relationships are in Red Hook. People <u>rely</u> on each other for <u>protection</u> and <u>support</u> — but "mix[ing] yourself with somebody else's family" can be <u>dangerous</u>.

4) Eddie's "*<u>fright</u> and <u>anger</u>*" suggests that the Liparis might be quite <u>dangerous</u>. Eddie's worried they might <u>harm</u> the Carbones: "They got a temper".

Theme — Honour

We see how <u>powerful</u> the ancient <u>codes</u> are when Eddie tries to help Marco and Rodolpho <u>escape</u> — he would rather let the man he <u>hates</u> go free than have the community find out that he <u>betrayed</u> them.

Remember to write about minor characters...

If it's relevant to the question, it's worth mentioning some of these extra characters in the exam. They represent the Italian American community in the play and help to show the wider impact of Eddie's actions.

Practice Questions

Now you've had a chance to get to know the Carbone family and a few of their neighbours, it's time to see how much you can remember. These questions are just to get you thinking — if there's something that you can't quite remember, have another read of this section.

Quick Questions

1) Why is Alfieri powerless to prevent the tragedy?

2) List three words that describe Eddie.

3) a) Give one example of affection in Eddie and Beatrice's marriage.
   b) Give one example of tension in Eddie and Beatrice's marriage.

4) Which two of these words best describe Beatrice's character?
   a) Selfish   b) Selfless   c) Interfering   d) Insightful

5) Name two of Catherine's characteristics which make her a good foil to Beatrice.

6) Give two pieces of evidence that show Catherine's instant attraction to Rodolpho.

7) Describe Rodolpho's appearance and character in a few words.

8) How does Rodolpho feel about being in America?

9) Why do the other dock workers admire Marco but make fun of Rodolpho?

10) Give three ways that Marco is similar to Eddie.

Practice Questions

For these questions you need to really think about your answer and use evidence from the text. Show me how brilliantly you've understood it all. Try to write about a paragraph for each question.

In-depth Questions

1) What is the effect of having Alfieri as a narrator?

2) What evidence is there that the respect of the community is important to Eddie?

3) Explain why Eddie might welcome death.

4) How successful do you think Beatrice is at resolving conflicts in the play?

5) Catherine takes Eddie's concerns about Rodolpho's motives seriously, even after Beatrice has told her to ignore them. Why do you think this is?

6) Do you think that Rodolpho loves Catherine, or does he just want citizenship? Explain your answer.

7) Why do you think Marco wants to be a good house guest?

8) Explain how Miller uses the wider Italian American community to show the effects of Eddie's betrayal.

Practice Questions

This time it's the real thing — well, almost. These questions are good practice for the exam, so it's worth doing them in exam-style conditions — that means without peeking back at this section too much. You'll need to write longer answers for these, too, so don't try doing them all at once — give yourself some time to work your magic, and then have a break — breaks are my favourite.

Exam-style Questions

1) To what extent is Eddie responsible for his own downfall, in your opinion? Refer to the text in your answer.

2) How does Miller present the character of Rodolpho in the play?

3) It is often said that Miller never judges the characters in his plays. Do you think that Miller's presentation of the characters in *A View from the Bridge* supports this view?

4) How does Miller's use of foils in *A View from the Bridge* develop the characters in the play?

5) Read the passage in Act One that begins "BEATRICE: Look, honey, you wanna get married..." to "CATHERINE: Okay."

   Explore how Miller uses this conversation between Beatrice and Catherine to give the audience an effective insight into both characters' personalities.

6) "When you have no wife you have dreams".
   To what extent is Marco's opinion supported by the relationships in the play?

Section Four — Themes

Love

Love is a powerful theme in the play — it drives people to do all sorts of things. Catherine loves Rodolpho, Rodolpho loves Catherine (probably), Marco loves his family and Eddie loves Beatrice... and Catherine.

There are three examples of romantic love in the play

1) Beatrice and Eddie are an example of when <u>married love</u> goes <u>wrong</u>:

- At the <u>beginning</u>, Beatrice and Eddie are <u>affectionate</u> towards each other.
- But they <u>argue</u> a lot and cannot <u>communicate</u> properly.
- They haven't <u>slept together</u> for "three months".
- Eddie's <u>last</u> words are "My B.!" — he only tries to <u>reconcile</u> their relationship as he dies.

2) <u>Marco</u> and his wife seem to have a strong relationship — he's "lonesome" and <u>misses</u> her, but <u>trusts</u> her while he is away. He's completely focused on <u>looking after</u> his wife and family.

3) When Catherine and Rodolpho meet they are <u>almost immediately attracted</u> to each other. They discuss their feelings much more <u>openly</u> than Eddie and Beatrice — "What worries you, Catherine?"

Family love is strong in Red Hook

© Donald Cooper/photostage.co.uk

1) Eddie and Beatrice took in Catherine as a <u>baby</u>, when her mother died. They now share a <u>parent-child</u> relationship.

2) Italian <u>immigrants</u> come to Red Hook to be near <u>family</u> — for example, Mr Lipari's <u>nephew</u> and Beatrice's <u>cousins</u>. The community is happy to <u>welcome</u> them — Beatrice takes in her cousins despite having <u>never</u> met them.

3) The two <u>brothers</u>, Marco and Rodolpho, <u>look out</u> for each other and seem to have always done everything <u>together</u>.

Eddie shows an unnatural love for Catherine

1) In the first scenes it might seem that Eddie is just <u>protective</u> of Catherine. But it becomes <u>clear</u> that he's also <u>possessive</u> of her — he says that Rodolpho's "<u>stealing</u>" by taking Catherine from him.

2) Alfieri and Beatrice both <u>warn</u> him about these feelings — Alfieri says that he has "<u>too much</u>" love for Catherine, but he doesn't <u>listen</u>.

3) Eddie doesn't want to <u>admit</u> that he has <u>inappropriate feelings</u> for Catherine:

- In a moment of drunken anger and frustration he "*<u>kisses</u> her on the mouth*".
- When Beatrice <u>confronts</u> him about his feelings Eddie is "*<u>horrified</u>, his fist clenching*" — he seems <u>disgusted</u> — he's never wanted to even consider these <u>feelings</u>.

Think about the different types of love in the play...

It's important to mention all the different types of love in the play, not just romantic love. For example, the love that characters have for their families is particularly strong — which leads me on to the next page...

Family

So, as promised, here's a page on family. Families stick together in Red Hook. Like most families, the Carbones have their issues — illegal immigrants, unnatural desires, knife fights. You know, the usual sort of thing...

Italian Americans put family first

1) One of the main reasons Red Hook was so popular with Italian immigrants was because many of their relatives had already settled there (see p.7).

2) They looked after and protected their families, even when it was illegal — Mrs Dondero and the Carbones both take in "submarines".

3) Family was the most important part of most Italian Americans' lives — "A man works, raises his family, goes bowling, eats, gets old, and then he dies."

© Rex/Alastair Muir

The Carbones are a typical Italian American family

The Carbones are a traditional Italian American family with traditional Italian American values:

- Eddie is the head of the family — he's hard-working, respected and protective of his niece.

- Beatrice is a housewife, she stays at home and cooks and cleans. She's always putting her family before herself and fussing about how the house looks.

- Catherine is like a daughter to the couple — she's obedient and eager to please. She listens to Beatrice and Eddie's advice and tries to please her 'parents' — "I'll do the dishes, B.!"

The family's problems get worse as the play progresses

Even though the family are close at the start of the play, there are already tensions. Beatrice is tired of Eddie's possessiveness of Catherine — "she's gotta go to work sometime."

↓

Beatrice tries to make them less of a family, reminding Eddie that Catherine is "no baby no more" and telling Catherine that Eddie isn't her father.

↓

Open conflict breaks out in the family after Catherine and Rodolpho start dating — Eddie's behaviour pushes Catherine away, and she's eventually forced to choose Rodolpho over her uncle.

↓

Eddie's call to Immigration is the last straw. The family bonds are broken and Catherine calls him a "rat!"

↓

But, Beatrice stays loyal to Eddie throughout the play and when Eddie is stabbed "The two women support him for a moment" — neither of them have really stopped caring for him.

"Even those who understand will turn against you"

Family loyalty is important in the play, which is why Eddie's betrayal is so serious. He's become the "Vinny" of the Carbone family — breaking his principles and his family. And I thought my house had dramas...

Honour

Eddie and Marco are men of honour — their actions are based on what they think is the right and honourable thing to do according to the laws of their community. They're like the knights of Red Hook...

Honour and reputation are important to Eddie and Marco

For Marco and Eddie, honour is a key part of their masculine identities and they'd do anything to protect it:

- They both care more about honour than they do the law.

- They think violence is an acceptable way to regain honour. For example, Eddie agrees with the treatment of Vinny Bolzano: "How's he gonna show his face?" (see p.11).

- The ending of the play is driven by their individual quests to regain their honour. Eddie thinks Marco's accusations have taken his "name" and Marco thinks Eddie's betrayal has taken away his honour.

> Miller was particularly interested in regaining your good name because his own reputation was damaged in 1957 by the HUAC (see p.1).

Character — Marco

Alfieri bails Marco because he promises not to harm Eddie: "You're an honorable man, I will believe your promise". However, for Marco, being honourable means taking revenge for the dishonour brought upon his family, not keeping a promise.

Eddie damages both Marco's honour and his own

1) Eddie is pushed to betray his family and his own values to get rid of Rodolpho.

2) In the play, betraying someone, particularly a family member, is perhaps the most dishonourable thing someone can do — Marco feels forced to take revenge on Eddie to protect his own honour.

3) Although he tries to blame Marco, it's Eddie's own act of betrayal which permanently ruins his reputation. He can't undo what he's done — proving "you can quicker get back a million dollars that was stole than a word that you gave away".

4) This means that only Marco is truly fighting for his family's honour, which has genuinely been tarnished by Eddie's betrayal.

Theme — Justice

It is possible that Marco triumphs over Eddie because he's fighting for true honour while Eddie is fighting for a reputation that he no longer deserves.

The pursuit of honour is destructive

1) Although honour is usually seen as a good trait, it leads to much of the play's violence, particularly the tragic conclusion.

2) Marco's quest for honour blinds him to reason. He not only destroys Eddie but also harms himself — he'll go to prison, and won't be able to look after his family.

3) Eddie's desire to salvage his reputation leads to his death. He has a *"strange sort of relaxation"* before the fight — maybe he'd rather die than live a life of dishonour.

© Continental Distributing Inc./Photofest

KEY QUOTE

"Nobody is gonna talk to him again if he lives to a hundred."

Once Eddie blows it, he really blows it. Catherine says that no-one will speak to him again, which is bad enough, but breaking the code of honour also leads to his death in a dramatic street brawl. Nasty.

Justice

Eddie and Marco both seek justice for things that they see as morally wrong, but aren't illegal —
this pushes them to take matters into their own hands, and we all know how that ends up...

There's a conflict between legal justice and community justice

The law determines legal justice, but the community has a different view of what's right. This is an idea
Alfieri introduces in the first scene — "There were many here who were justly shot by unjust men":

1) It's illegal for Marco and Rodolpho to enter the country without permission
   — but it goes against the law of the community to report them.

2) Vinny reports his family's illegal activity to Immigration, but he faces community
   justice because he betrayed his family — people "spit on him in the street".

3) Eddie is within the law when he reports the cousins — but Marco believes
   "All the law is not in a book" and that Eddie deserves to be punished.

Alfieri is a mediator between the two types of justice

1) Alfieri plays a role traditionally played by a priest in plays — the characters visit him for advice, but
   unlike a priest he provides a more balanced view of justice — not just from a religious perspective.

2) Alfieri recognises the distinction between the two types of justice:

   - He knows the law is limited — "When the law is wrong
     it's because it's unnatural". He believes that "Only God
     makes justice", it isn't the community's responsibility.
     The law and natural justice are separate ideas for Alfieri.

   - He understands that community justice is very
     powerful — he warns Eddie against calling
     Immigration, even though it's legally right, because
     he wouldn't "have a friend in the world".

   - He realises that both have their place in society, but
     thinks it's better to "settle for half" — justice by the law.

*Community justice and legal
justice don't always match
up in the play — this leads
to conflict and violence.*

Writer's Techniques

Alfieri symbolises a bridge
between the two types of justice.
He exists between the Italian
and American cultures — he
understands both and tries to
find a balance between them.

Marco and Eddie seek their own justice

1) Unlike Alfieri, Marco and Eddie struggle to understand the two types of justice:

   - Marco can't understand why, in America, "There is no other law" except what's in a book.

   - Eddie can't understand that Alfieri can only "deal in what's provable"
     — there is no law against Rodolpho and Catherine's marriage.

2) They both believe that people should be punished for their
   perceived crimes, so they dish out their own justice.

Write about how different characters understand justice...

Justice is a great theme to write about in the exam. Everyone in the play has got their own idea of what's
right and wrong. Ultimately everyone wants justice, though, which is what leads to the play's tragic ending.

Men and Women

The differences between the older and younger generations show that the characters in the play aren't just gender stereotypes. I'm not even sure they had stereotypes in the 1950s — I thought they had record players...

The men have traditional beliefs about masculinity

1) Both Eddie and Marco are <u>hard-working</u> family men. Marco in particular has characteristics that were traditionally associated with <u>manliness</u> — he lets his <u>actions</u> do the talking and is as <u>strong</u> as a "bull".

2) Eddie and the other workers think Rodolpho is <u>strange</u> because he isn't 'manly'. Eddie thinks Rodolpho might be <u>gay</u> because he <u>looks</u> and <u>behaves</u> in a way that was traditionally considered <u>feminine</u>:

- He likes buying new <u>clothes</u> ("Shoes. Jackets.") and Eddie <u>suspects</u> that he <u>dyes</u> his hair blond ("I just hope that's his regular hair").
- He <u>sings</u>, <u>sews</u> and <u>cooks</u> — Eddie says that someone who can do these things <u>shouldn't</u> be working at the docks, which <u>implies</u> that he <u>doesn't</u> think he's 'manly' enough to be a longshoreman.

Beatrice and Catherine are typical 1950s women

1) The women in the play both follow Eddie's <u>rules</u> in the household, even if they don't <u>agree</u> with them. They are generally more <u>talkative</u> and <u>sensitive</u> than the men.

2) Beatrice is a <u>stereotypical</u> housewife. She's loyal, respectful, and <u>cares</u> for the family: "I'll make the fish." Catherine is also keen to <u>please</u> her partner, Rodolpho: "You hungry?"

3) Beatrice has "<u>never</u> worked" outside the house. However, Catherine wants to follow a <u>different</u> path — she wants to be more <u>independent</u> and go out to <u>work</u>.

4) Yet both women seem to perceive <u>marriage</u> as the <u>main focus</u> in life — once Catherine develops a <u>relationship</u> with Rodolpho she gets <u>distracted</u> from her ambition to be a <u>stenographer</u> — she stops practising.

> Marco claims that "When you have <u>no wife</u> you have <u>dreams</u>". This also seems to apply to having a husband — once Catherine is dating Rodolpho, her dreams seem <u>less important</u>.

There is a power struggle in Eddie and Beatrice's marriage

1) Although Beatrice is a <u>stereotypical</u> housewife, she does fight Eddie for <u>power</u> in their <u>relationship</u>. She <u>confronts</u> him about Catherine, and <u>challenges</u> him about the state of their relationship.

2) She questions Eddie's <u>manliness</u> when she says "When am I gonna be a wife again". This really <u>hurts</u> Eddie, who <u>refuses</u> to deal with the issue.

© Tristram Kenton/Lebrecht Music & Arts

3) After the cousins have <u>moved</u> out, Beatrice is <u>angry</u> with Eddie, but he throws his weight around demanding "<u>respect</u>". He thinks she should <u>support</u> him, whether she <u>agrees</u> or not.

4) He tries to take back <u>power</u> by giving her an <u>ultimatum</u>, and manages to stop her going to the wedding.

Mention which characters fit gender stereotypes...

If you're asked to write about men and women in the exam, don't forget to consider a variety of characters from the play. Think about gender stereotypes and compare the main characters to them. Simples...

Sexuality

Sexuality is a theme that crops up in a fair few places throughout the play. It's mainly associated with Catherine — her growing sexuality doesn't go unmissed by the men, and it certainly causes Beatrice a lot of stress.

Eddie's relationships have become confused

1) Eddie seems to have <u>transferred</u> his <u>sexual</u> feelings for Beatrice to Catherine, causing <u>problems</u> in their marriage:

Eddie and Beatrice

- Eddie and Beatrice don't have <u>sex</u> anymore. Beatrice <u>worries</u> that he's no longer attracted to her but he <u>won't talk</u> about it.
- They struggle to <u>talk</u> about what has gone wrong and seem to be <u>drifting</u> apart.

Eddie and Catherine

- Eddie has an <u>unnatural love</u> for Catherine — he has "too much love" and has become <u>sexually</u> attracted to her.
- Eddie tries to <u>control</u> Catherine's <u>sexuality</u> — telling her not to be "so <u>friendly</u>", and by telling her what to <u>wear</u>.
- When Catherine lights Eddie's <u>cigar</u> in Act One, it could be a <u>symbol</u> of his <u>sexual</u> feelings for her (see p.50).

2) Eddie seems unaware of his <u>unnatural</u> feelings for Catherine — he's "*horrified*" when faced with the truth.

Catherine is becoming a woman

1) <u>Being a woman</u> and <u>sexuality</u> are connected in the play:

- Beatrice doesn't think she's a "<u>wife</u>" when Eddie stops sleeping with her.
- Beatrice corrects Catherine's inadvertent <u>sexual behaviour</u> to make her realise she has to <u>grow up</u>.
- Catherine is presented as becoming a "grown <u>woman</u>" because she's in a <u>relationship</u>. Her behaviour in the play becomes <u>increasingly sexual</u>, and she eventually <u>sleeps with</u> Rodolpho.

© Rex/Alastair Muir

2) This is partly why Eddie tries to <u>control</u> Catherine's sexuality — he doesn't want her to grow up. However, he can't stop her having a <u>sexual relationship</u> with Rodolpho.

Eddie's kiss with Rodolpho is ambiguous

The scene where Eddie <u>kisses</u> Rodolpho is very <u>significant</u> because it's so <u>ambiguous</u>. It could mean...

This same-sex kiss would have been particularly shocking to a 1950s audience — homosexuality was viewed differently compared to today.

- Eddie is trying to show Catherine that Rodolpho is <u>gay</u> (see p.40).
- He's trying to <u>impress</u> Catherine by showing her he's the <u>dominant</u> male.
- He's trying to take back Catherine's <u>virginity</u> from Rodolpho by <u>kissing</u> the man who kissed her.

 KEY QUOTE

"When am I gonna be a wife again, Eddie?"

Eddie and Beatrice drift further apart as the play continues, whilst Catherine and Rodolpho grow closer. Catherine's growing sexuality highlights the absence of a sexual relationship between Beatrice and Eddie.

Conflict

Plays are all about conflict — if everything was hunky-dory it wouldn't be half as interesting to watch. I saw a brilliant example of conflict at a theatre once. It was during the interval, in the queue for refreshments...

Eddie's feelings for Catherine cause conflicts

1) Eddie's <u>confused</u> feelings for Catherine cause a conflict within <u>himself</u> — he can't <u>accept</u> them and <u>refuses</u> to talk about it when Alfieri <u>suggests</u> the possibility: "What're you talkin' about".

2) Beatrice is <u>aware</u> of how Eddie feels, and his lack of <u>interest</u> in her causes <u>arguments</u> between them: "I got nothin' to say about it!"

3) There are <u>hints</u> of conflict between Catherine and Beatrice. Catherine thinks that Beatrice is always "goin' at" Eddie and doesn't <u>understand</u> him — she <u>blames</u> Beatrice for Eddie being unhappy. Beatrice also seems to harbour some <u>resentment</u> towards Catherine for causing her marital <u>problems</u> — "you should have thought of it before".

© Donald Cooper/photostage.co.uk

4) Eddie's feelings also cause conflict between him and Catherine as he becomes increasingly <u>controlling</u>. When Eddie stops Rodolpho singing, it provokes Catherine's <u>first disagreement</u> with him — "Leave him finish" — a sign of more <u>disagreements</u> to come.

The conflicts between the men are unspoken

1) There are just <u>small signs</u> that Eddie <u>dislikes</u> Rodolpho at first — he's <u>abrupt</u> when Rodolpho speaks to him: "for Christ's sake".

2) When Eddie punches Rodolpho in a <u>boxing lesson</u>, it <u>warns</u> Rodolpho that Eddie's <u>stronger</u> than him. However, this remains <u>unsaid</u> and Eddie <u>pretends</u> it was just a lesson.

3) Marco steps in to <u>protect</u> his brother and also uses <u>actions</u> rather than words — he "raises the <u>chair</u> over his head" (see p.13).

4) It's only after Eddie believes that Catherine and Rodolpho have <u>slept together</u>, that the <u>conflict</u> between the men <u>comes out</u> into the open.

It's difficult to keep conflicts private in Red Hook

1) The Red Hook community is very <u>close</u>, so private conflicts often <u>spill</u> out into <u>public</u>:

- Eddie's conflict with Rodolpho becomes public when Eddie calls <u>Immigration</u>. This is partly due to Marco's public <u>accusations</u> and also because Eddie accidentally involves other members of the <u>community</u> — the two <u>new immigrants</u> are also arrested.

- Eddie also confronts Marco in <u>public</u> when he tries to regain his <u>reputation</u>.

2) The final conflict in the play is presented by Alfieri. He has a <u>personal</u> conflict between his <u>public</u> and <u>private</u> feelings. Publicly, he should <u>condemn</u> Eddie's betrayal, but privately he can't help but "<u>love</u>" him.

Mention how conflict creates dramatic moments in the play...

When it comes down to it, conflict is the driving force behind pretty much every single great (and not so great) dramatic work ever written. Show that you understand how conflict drives the plot of the play.

Practice Questions

So there you have it, you're probably pretty familiar with the key themes in 'A View from the Bridge' by now. They're not too bad once you get the hang of them, but it might help to look back at the play with the themes in mind — make yourself an expert on who says what and when. Then, have a go at these quick questions to see how much you remember.

Quick Questions

1) Give an example from the play of:
   a) Romantic love   b) Family love   c) Unnatural love

2) What is Eddie talking about when he says that Rodolpho is "stealing" from him?

3) Give two pieces of evidence from the play that show the audience that family is important in Red Hook.

4) Briefly explain why the Carbones seem like a typical 1950s family.

5) Which two characters are most obsessed with honour?

6) Who does Eddie blame for damaging his honour? Who is actually responsible?

7) Briefly describe the difference between legal justice and community justice.

8) According to the play:
   a) How were men meant to act in the 1950s?
   b) How were women meant to act in the 1950s?

9) Give two pieces of evidence from the play that show Catherine is becoming a woman.

10) What is the key conflict which drives the play's main action?

Practice Questions

These questions will take you a little bit longer — try to include a few points for each one. Make sure you refer to the text to show that you've understood it, and give any personal opinions that you have.

In-depth Questions

1) Do you think that Eddie is aware of his unnatural feelings towards Catherine? Give reasons to support your answer.

2) Do you think that Eddie is still loved by his family at the end of the play?

3) In your opinion, is honour presented negatively in *A View from the Bridge*?

4) Why is it so important for Eddie to get back his "name" in front of the community?

5) Explain how legal justice and community justice come into conflict during the play.

6) Do you believe that Eddie feels he is doing the right thing when he reports Marco and Rodolpho to Immigration? Why?

7) Why do you think Miller makes Rodolpho's sexuality ambiguous?

8) Why do you think Eddie kisses Rodolpho? Give reasons for your answer.

Practice Questions

Time for everyone's favourite — exam-style questions... Well, examiners like them, so it's a good idea to get as much practice as you can. Remember to do these in exam-style conditions, too — then you'll be super prepared for the real thing.

Exam-style Questions

1) *"A View from the Bridge* is about unnatural love". How far would you agree with this assessment of the play?

2) Read the passage in Act One, just after Beatrice walks on stage, beginning "BEATRICE: *in the face of Catherine's shout...*" and ending "Go, Baby, set the table."

   Explore how Miller makes this scene an insight into the workings of a traditional Italian American family.

3) "The law? All the law is not in a book."
   How does Miller present issues concerning justice and law in *A View from the Bridge*?

4) Read the passage at the start of Act Two, which begins "RODOLPHO: *steps closer to her*" and ends "And don't cry anymore."

   How does Miller make this scene a significant moment for Catherine in the play?

5) How does Miller present the differences between men and women in *A View from the Bridge*?

6) "Eddie is the source of all conflicts in *A View from the Bridge*."
   How far do you agree with this assessment of the play?

Section Four — Themes

'A View from the Bridge' On the Stage

I always thought those pesky stage directions just interrupted the action, but it turns out that they do a pretty good job of telling you what the stage performance of *A View from the Bridge* should be like.

The set traps the characters in the action

1) Miller states that *"The main acting area"* should be the *"living room — dining room"*. This keeps the focus on the increasing tensions inside the flat. The major characters are trapped together — maximising potential conflicts.

A room that makes you feel trapped in a small space is described as 'claustrophobic'.

2) Miller's design helps make the play's atmosphere seem more claustrophobic and intense.

3) Alfieri is the only one who isn't trapped. His desk, representing his office, is *"forestage"* — it's between the main scene of action and the audience, suggesting that he is part-actor and part-spectator.

Stage directions help shape the characters

1) Miller uses stage directions to give the audience an insight into the characters:

- From the first time we see Beatrice — *"wiping her hands with a towel"* — she is usually doing household chores. This shows that she is always doing things for her family.

- The family cross themselves before eating. This religious gesture hints that they have stayed true to traditional Italian beliefs — Italians are traditionally Catholics.

- We can tell that Eddie doesn't like discussing his marital problems with Beatrice when he is *"in retreat"* before she's even got to the point.

2) Stage directions also tell us how the characters interact with each other, e.g. Catherine talks to Eddie while *"taking his arm"* — this shows they have an affectionate relationship.

A private tragedy plays out in public

1) Most of the play takes place in the private setting of the Carbones' home, but the audience can always see the rest of the street on stage. The flat is connected by a *"stairway... to the next story"* and *"Ramps"* represent the street. This shows that they are closely surrounded by the community.

2) Miller includes the street in the set to make the consequences of Eddie's actions clear. The play is about private conflicts within a family, but Eddie causes these private conflicts to spill out into public — his actions affect the wider community, like the Liparis.

3) The street is where Marco accuses Eddie of betrayal, and where the play's final confrontation takes place. It means that all of Red Hook knows what's happened in the Carbone family and community justice appropriately plays out in public.

© Roger-Viollet / Topfoto

EXAM TIP

Think about how the play might be performed...

When you're discussing the text, remember it was written to be performed. If you've never seen it acted out, maybe you could have a go yourself — I like pretending to be Marco, but I just can't get that chair trick right...

The Structure of 'A View from the Bridge'

AVFTB's like a roller coaster — you spend ages going uphill, gradually building tension, then suddenly things quickly spiral downwards and out of control. And then you leave wishing you hadn't eaten so many sweets...

'A View from the Bridge' is a modern Greek tragedy

Miller originally wrote the play as a <u>Greek tragedy</u>, with all the dialogue in <u>verse</u>. He later <u>revised</u> the play into its current form, but the play still shares similarities with a <u>Greek tragedy</u>:

A Greek Tragedy

- A <u>chorus</u> gives <u>background</u> information and helps the audience <u>interpret</u> events. It also warns them of what is to come.

- They centre on a <u>tragic hero</u> with a <u>fatal flaw</u> — his own actions cause his <u>downfall</u>.

- The <u>ending</u> in a Greek tragedy is <u>inevitable</u>.

A View from the Bridge

- As an <u>educated</u> narrator with the gift of <u>hindsight</u>, <u>Alfieri</u> plays the role of the Greek chorus.

- You could argue that Eddie's fatal flaw is <u>denial</u> — he can't accept the <u>truth</u> and loses control. His <u>downfall</u> is a result of <u>him</u> calling Immigration — it's all his own <u>fault</u>.

- Alfieri says that the <u>outcome</u> of Eddie's story seemed <u>inevitable</u> — "I could see every step coming".

There are only two acts in 'A View from the Bridge'

1) Miller's original version of the play only had <u>one act</u>. He wanted "<u>continuous action</u>", so he set the play in <u>one location</u> (the Carbone's flat), only had a <u>few characters</u>, and everything happened in a <u>short space of time</u>. When Miller rewrote the play as <u>two acts</u>, he kept these features to create <u>tension</u> and <u>drama</u>.

2) Two act plays usually have a similar <u>structure</u>:

   - The <u>first act</u> is <u>longer</u>, and <u>develops</u> the conflict of the play. It usually ends on a <u>climax</u> to leave the audience <u>curious</u> about what's going to happen. In *A View from the Bridge* this is the <u>chair-lifting</u> scene — Eddie's <u>authority</u> has been challenged and the audience <u>wonder</u> how he'll react.

   - The <u>second act</u> is usually much <u>shorter</u> as things speed towards a conclusion — the <u>audience</u> usually has an <u>idea</u> of how the play will end from the events in the first act. In *A View from the Bridge*, both acts end in <u>confrontation</u> between <u>Marco</u> and <u>Eddie</u>.

These events will happen again

1) One of the reasons Miller originally wrote the play as a <u>Greek tragedy</u> is because he thought Eddie's story was <u>timeless</u> — it's a series of events that <u>keeps happening</u>.

2) Many of the events in the play also keep happening — they're <u>cyclical</u>. The story of Vinny Bolzano <u>warns</u> us of what is going to happen. Even some <u>details</u> are the same — the family "<u>spit</u> on" Vinny, and Marco later "<u>spits</u> into Eddie's face".

3) Alfieri even wonders in his first speech whether other lawyers in <u>history</u> have "heard the <u>same complaint</u> and sat there as <u>powerless</u> as [him]".

4) <u>Miller's</u> message could be that you can't change <u>human nature</u>. People will <u>always</u> <u>betray</u> each other and seek <u>revenge</u> — the <u>law</u> can't do anything to prevent it.

"I knew where he was going to end."

Impress the examiner by saying that Eddie is a tragic hero — he's doomed from the start. Alfieri "knew" that things would end badly for Eddie, but he's powerless to stop it. He can only watch as it all goes pear-shaped.

Language in 'A View from the Bridge'

What you say is one thing, but how you say it is really important too — remember that next time you have to explain to your teacher that your dog's eaten your homework...

The characters use everyday language

© Tristram Kenton/Lebrecht Music & Arts

1) The characters' lines are written in a <u>natural</u> way — they use the type of language that people <u>really used</u> in 1950s New York.

2) They <u>interrupt</u> one another, get <u>distracted</u> and lose the thread of the conversation. For example, in the first scene, Catherine is <u>speaking</u> to Eddie one moment, and the next she's <u>calling</u> to Beatrice.

3) When they want to <u>emphasise</u> a point, they often <u>repeat</u> themselves — like when <u>Eddie</u> goes on about how Rodolpho "sings" and "cooks".

4) As with real people, the audience has to <u>read between the lines</u> to work out what the characters really mean. When Eddie says that Rodolpho "<u>ain't right</u>" — what he means is he thinks Rodolpho's <u>gay</u>.

Miller uses local speech to set the scene

1) Miller uses <u>dialogue</u> to mimic the way Italian Americans would've talked in <u>1950s Brooklyn</u>. He makes it realistic by using:

- <u>dialect words</u> — he uses <u>local</u> working-class words and <u>phrases</u> — for example "<u>submarines</u>" (meaning illegal immigrants) and saying "<u>I mean</u>" at the end of sentences.

- <u>non-standard spelling</u> — Miller describes how words should be <u>pronounced</u> by <u>spelling</u> words <u>differently</u> such as "<u>gonna</u>" instead of "going to" and "<u>yiz</u>" instead of 'you'.

- <u>omission</u> — letters are <u>missed off</u> words and replaced with an <u>apostrophe</u> to show how the words would've sounded such as "walkin'", "nothin'", "burnin'".

2) Marco and Rodolpho speak fairly good <u>English</u>, but occasionally they say things like, "Everybody waits only for the train". The meaning is clear, but the word order is slightly <u>odd</u> — reminding the audience that English isn't their <u>first language</u>.

3) Miller uses <u>ordinary speech</u> because he wants the audience to understand that although the story is <u>fictional</u>, the events and characters are realistic (and timeless) — this could've happened to <u>any</u> family.

Alfieri speaks in Standard English

1) Alfieri doesn't speak with a <u>dialect</u>, which sets him <u>apart</u> from the key characters. It makes him seem <u>educated</u> and gives his words more <u>authority</u>.

2) His language is often <u>poetic</u>. He uses <u>metaphors</u> such as, "This is the gullet of New York", to paint a vivid <u>picture</u> of Red Hook.

3) These <u>language features</u> remind the audience that Alfieri is slightly <u>detached</u> from the play's action — he's not like the rest of the locals — he's both an <u>observer</u> and a <u>character</u>.

Language in 'A View from the Bridge'

We learn a lot about the characters through the way they speak. I find it helpful to read the play using a different voice for each character — plus I've got a beautiful wig that I wear when I'm playing Catherine...

Eddie uses simple, direct language

1) Eddie's language is <u>direct</u> and to the point:

- He uses <u>unsophisticated</u> vocabulary — this means what he says is quite <u>simplistic</u>. He seems unable to <u>develop</u> his thoughts — probably why he can't <u>come to terms</u> with his confused feelings for Catherine.

- He's a man of <u>few words</u> — he speaks in <u>short</u> sentences and <u>repeats</u> himself. This makes his speech <u>powerful</u> because he only says what he thinks needs to be said.

- He's <u>aggressive</u> — his desire to <u>control</u> people means he cuts people off, responds to questions with <u>close-ended answers</u> (he doesn't expand on what he's saying) or just <u>refuses</u> to talk at all: "I got nothin' to say about it!"

2) However, Eddie's language is occasionally very <u>expressive</u>. For example when he says you could <u>blow Rodolpho over</u> "if you close the paper fast".

Catherine's language changes throughout the play

1) In the first act Catherine doesn't seem very confident — often turning statements into <u>questions</u>, e.g. "I'll get you a beer, all right?" — she's <u>unsure</u> of herself and wants <u>approval</u>.

2) She also talks in quite a <u>childish</u> way, which emphasises her <u>innocence</u>. She exclaims <u>excitedly</u> at unexpected things, such as the fact that Rodolpho is "practically <u>blond</u>!" and when she imagines <u>lemon trees</u> in Italy.

©Nigel Norrington / ArenaPAL

3) However, by the end of the play Catherine speaks with <u>passion</u> and <u>confidence</u>, calling Eddie a "rat" who belongs in the "garbage". This is a strong <u>contrast</u> with the Catherine of Act One.

Language is a key difference between the cousins

1) Rodolpho's <u>friendly</u>, <u>chatty</u> and <u>light-hearted</u>. He even responds to simple requests with <u>enthusiasm</u>: "Sugar? Yes! I like it very much!" His <u>willingness</u> to talk <u>contrasts</u> with Eddie and Marco. He's open and speaks to Catherine with <u>affection</u> while Eddie tries to hide his feelings.

2) Despite English not being Rodolpho's <u>first language</u>, he uses <u>poetic</u> and <u>colourful</u> language, such as when he compares Catherine to a "<u>little bird</u>".

3) Marco says even less than Eddie — he doesn't <u>need</u> to talk to show his <u>superiority</u> — he's silent when he lifts the chair, but the <u>meaning is clear</u>. The only time Marco really says anything is in the <u>final scenes</u> — this makes his <u>anger</u> seem even more <u>powerful</u>.

Write about what language tells us about the characters...

You could write that Miller uses each character's speech to tell the audience about their lives — for example, even without any background info, an audience could tell that Alfieri was better educated than, say, Eddie.

Symbolism in 'A View from the Bridge'

I absolutely love a bit of symbolism, it's my favourite piece of percussion. The way that sound echoes around the room — oh, wait, no. Those are cymbals. Well, I guess symbolism's pretty good too...

The Brooklyn Bridge is the bridge in the title

1) The Brooklyn Bridge connects Red Hook, a "slum" in Brooklyn (in the 1950s), to the wealthy New York island of Manhattan.

2) Alfieri makes a good narrator because his view is 'symbolically' the view from the bridge. He can see things from the Italian immigrants' perspective in Red Hook, but also from the American perspective in Manhattan. He is the bridge between the two communities:

©iStockphoto.com/groveb

- He understands the immigrants' ideas about honour and justice because he grew up with the old Italian ways, moving to America when he was twenty-five.

- BUT he understands how justice works in America as he's a qualified lawyer.

The American Dream was the idea that America was a place where anyone could achieve anything, regardless of their background.

3) The bridge is also a symbol of opportunity — to cross the bridge and become part of the wealthy, glamorous area of Manhattan is to fulfil the American Dream. This is why Rodolpho is so keen to go to Broadway — he wants to live the American Dream and be "something wonderful".

The dagger symbolises jealousy and betrayal

1) Daggers are often considered as symbols of deception and betrayal — to stab someone with a dagger you have to get close to them, which an enemy wouldn't normally let you do.

2) It might also symbolise jealousy, as jealous people sometimes feel as if they're being stabbed in the heart.

3) Marco kills Eddie with his own knife — it symbolises that Eddie's killed by his own jealousy and treachery.

Symbols of sexuality appear throughout the play

The song 'Paper Doll' is also symbolic of Eddie's feelings for Catherine — it's about loving someone who's not yours to love.

1) Catherine's increasing awareness of her sexuality is symbolised throughout the play — most obviously by her high-heels:

- The high-heels show Catherine's ready to become a woman. She likes wearing them because it makes men's heads turn "like windmills" — they give her power over men.

- Eddie hates her wearing them because they show she's growing up and ready to start dating. He might also be worried about the unnatural feelings they could arouse in him.

2) The scene in Act One where Catherine lights Eddie's cigar is often seen as symbolic — the cigar is seen as a phallic symbol, and the scene suggests that Catherine 'lights Eddie's fire'. It also shows Catherine is taking on the traditional role of a wife by taking care of Eddie.

Show that you understand why these symbols are included...

Symbols like these don't just appear by accident — Miller includes them deliberately in order to convey a deeper message. Make sure you explore their meaning fully if you mention them in your exam answer.

Practice Questions

Surprise, surprise, I've got some more questions for you. They shouldn't be too tricky — you're probably an expert by now. Also, there's no point in learning all this stuff if you can't prove it by boasting about how you got all the answers right...

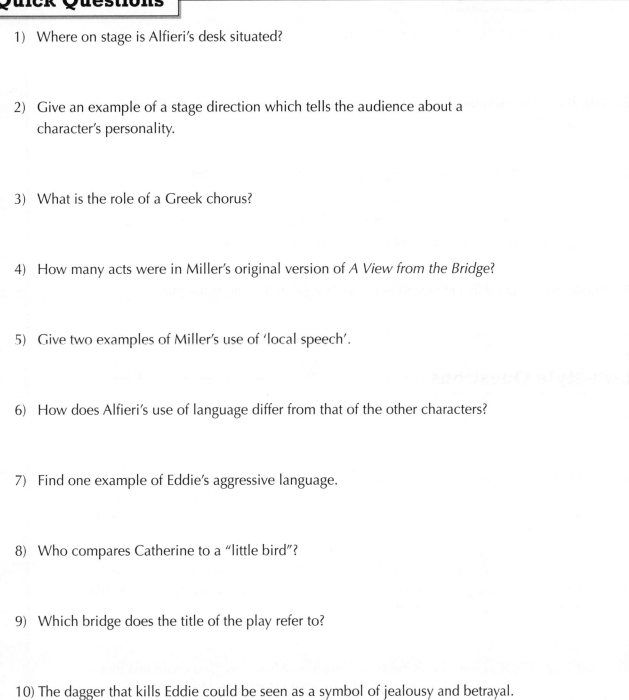

Quick Questions

1) Where on stage is Alfieri's desk situated?

2) Give an example of a stage direction which tells the audience about a character's personality.

3) What is the role of a Greek chorus?

4) How many acts were in Miller's original version of *A View from the Bridge*?

5) Give two examples of Miller's use of 'local speech'.

6) How does Alfieri's use of language differ from that of the other characters?

7) Find one example of Eddie's aggressive language.

8) Who compares Catherine to a "little bird"?

9) Which bridge does the title of the play refer to?

10) The dagger that kills Eddie could be seen as a symbol of jealousy and betrayal. Give one other example of symbolism in the play.

Practice Questions

These are the last in-depth and exam-style questions in the whole book — is that a cry of relief I hear? You know what to do by now — so set a timer and make this last practice worthwhile. Remember to be as analytical as you can, and don't forget to include quotes from the text.

In-depth Questions

1) Why do you think that Miller chose to set key parts of the play's action outside of the Carbones' flat?

2) Why do you think Miller's two-act version of the play was more popular than his original play?

3) What does Catherine's changing language tell us about her character?

4) Explain how Marco and Rodolpho's different characters are reflected in the way they speak. Support your argument with examples from the text.

5) Briefly explain the different meanings of the 'bridge' in the title of the play.

Exam-style Questions

1) How does the set design help build tension in the play?

2) Read from "EDDIE *in thought sits in his chair*..." to the end of Act One, and from "MARCO: Eddie Carbone!" to the end of Act Two. Compare and contrast the endings of both Acts. How far does Miller prepare the audience for the play's climax through the ending of Act One?

3) "Miller's use of language makes the characters in *A View from the Bridge* come to life." To what extent do you agree with this statement?

4) Read from "EDDIE: I see it in his eyes; he's laughin' at her..." to "you could kiss him he was so sweet" in the middle of Act One. To what extent does Miller's use of language in this passage help the audience to empathise with Eddie?

5) Explore how the use of symbolism allows Miller to create different layers of meaning in *A View from the Bridge*.

Exam Preparation

Getting to know the text will put you at a massive advantage in the exam. It's not enough just to read it though — you've got to get to grips with the nitty-gritty bits. It's all about gathering evidence...

The exam questions will test three main skills

You will need to show the examiner that you can:

1) Write about the play in a <u>thoughtful way</u> — <u>picking out</u> appropriate <u>examples</u> and <u>quotations</u> to back up your opinions.

2) <u>Identify</u> and <u>explain</u> features of the play's <u>form</u>, <u>structure</u> and <u>language</u>. Show how Miller uses these to present the <u>ideas</u>, <u>themes</u>, <u>characters</u> and <u>settings</u> effectively.

3) Write in a <u>clear</u>, <u>well-structured</u> way. <u>5%</u> of the marks in your English Literature exams are for <u>spelling</u>, <u>punctuation</u> and <u>grammar</u>. Make sure that your writing is as <u>accurate</u> as possible.

Preparation is important

1) It's <u>important</u> to cover <u>all</u> the <u>different sections</u> of this book in your <u>revision</u>. You need to make sure you <u>understand</u> the text's <u>context</u>, <u>plot</u>, <u>characters</u>, <u>themes</u> and <u>writer's techniques</u>.

2) In the <u>exam</u>, you'll need to <u>bring together</u> your <u>ideas</u> about these topics to answer the question <u>quickly</u>.

3) Think about the different <u>characters</u> and <u>themes</u> in the text, and write down some <u>key points</u> and <u>ideas</u> about each one. Then, find some <u>evidence</u> to support each point — this could be something from <u>any</u> of the <u>sections</u> in this book. You could set out your evidence in a <u>table</u> like this:

Theme: Love	
Romantic love	Catherine and Rodolpho, Marco and his wife — examples of devoted romantic relationships.
Beatrice and Eddie	Romantic love gone wrong — they argue and no longer have sex. Eddie's last words ("My B.!"). Beatrice's loyalty to him.
Family love	Eddie and Beatrice look after Catherine. Marco and Rodolpho's relationship. The dishonour of betraying your family.
Unnatural love	Suggestion that Eddie's love for Catherine is inappropriate. Also homosexuality — Eddie thinks it "ain't right".
Driving force	Love drives the plot — Eddie's love for Catherine and Marco's love for Rodolpho both cause conflict/motivate characters to act.

Preparing to succeed — a cunning plot indeed...

Knowing the plot inside out will be unbelievably helpful in the exam. It'll help you to stay calm and make sure you write a brilliant answer that positively glitters with little gems of evidence. The exam's just a chance for you to show off...

The Exam Question

This page deals with how to approach an exam question. The stuff below will help you get started on a scorching exam answer, more scorching than, say, a phoenix cooking fiery fajitas in a flaming furnace.

Read the question carefully and underline key words

1) The style of question you'll get depends on which <u>exam board</u> you're taking.

2) Read all the <u>instructions</u> carefully. Make sure you know <u>how many</u> questions you need to answer and <u>how much time</u> you should spend answering each one.

3) If the question has <u>more than one part</u>, look at the total number of marks for each bit. This should help you to plan your <u>time</u> in the exam.

4) <u>Read</u> the question at least <u>twice</u> so you completely understand it. <u>Underline</u> the key words. If you're given an <u>extract</u>, underline <u>important</u> words or phrases in that too.

Henry didn't read the weather report carefully enough when planning his weekend activities.

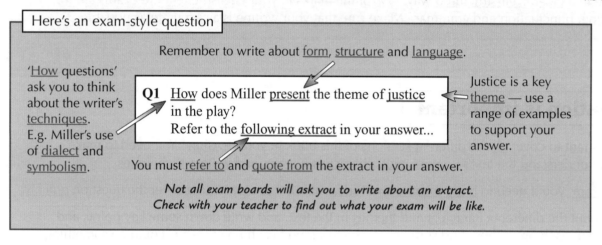

Here's an exam-style question

Remember to write about <u>form</u>, <u>structure</u> and <u>language</u>.

'<u>How</u> questions' ask you to think about the writer's <u>techniques</u>. E.g. Miller's use of <u>dialect</u> and <u>symbolism</u>.

Q1 <u>How</u> does Miller <u>present</u> the theme of <u>justice</u> in the play?
Refer to the <u>following extract</u> in your answer...

Justice is a key <u>theme</u> — use a range of examples to support your answer.

You must <u>refer to</u> and <u>quote from</u> the extract in your answer.

Not all exam boards will ask you to write about an extract.
Check with your teacher to find out what your exam will be like.

Get to know exam language

Some <u>words</u> come up time and again in <u>exam questions</u>. Have a look at some <u>specimen</u> questions, pick out words that are <u>often used</u> in questions and make sure that you <u>understand</u> what they mean. You could <u>write a few down</u> whilst you're revising. For example:

Question Word	You need to...
Explore / Explain	Show <u>how</u> the writer deals with a <u>theme</u>, <u>character</u> or <u>idea</u>. Make several <u>different</u> points to answer the question.
How does	Think about the <u>techniques</u> or <u>literary features</u> that the author uses to get their point across.
Give examples	Use <u>direct quotes</u> and describe <u>events</u> from the text in your own words.
Refer to	Read the question so that you know if you need to write about just an <u>extract</u>, or an extract and the <u>rest of the text</u>.

The advice squad — the best cops in the NYPD...

Whatever question you're asked in the exam, your answer should touch on the main characters, themes, structure and language of the text. All the stuff we've covered in the rest of the book in fact. It's so neat, it's almost like we planned it.

Planning Your Answer

I'll say this once — and then I'll probably repeat it several times — it is absolutely, completely, totally and utterly essential that you make a plan before you start writing. Only a fool jumps right in without a plan...

Plan your answer before you start

1) If you plan, you're less likely to forget something <u>important</u>.

2) A good plan will help you <u>organise</u> your ideas — and write a good, <u>well-structured</u> essay.

3) Write your plan at the <u>top of your answer booklet</u> and draw a <u>neat line</u> through it when you've finished.

4) <u>Don't</u> spend <u>too long</u> on your plan. It's only <u>rough work</u>, so you don't need to write in full sentences. Here are a few <u>examples</u> of different ways you can plan your answer:

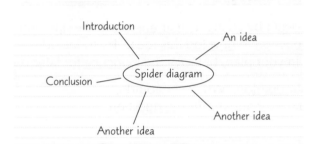

Bullet points...

* Introduction...
* An idea...
* The next idea...
* Another idea...
* Yet another idea...
* Conclusion...

Include bits of evidence in your plan

1) <u>Writing</u> your essay will be much <u>easier</u> if you include <u>important quotes</u> and <u>examples</u> in your plan.

2) You could include them in a <u>table</u> like this one:

3) <u>Don't</u> spend <u>too long</u> writing out quotes though. It's just to make sure you <u>don't forget</u> anything when you write your answer.

A point...	Quote to back this up...
Another point...	Quote...
A different point...	Example...
A brand new point...	Quote...

Structure your answer

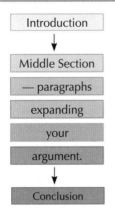

Introduction
↓
Middle Section
— paragraphs
expanding
your
argument.
↓
Conclusion

1) Your <u>introduction</u> should give a brief answer to the question you're writing about. Make it clear how you're going to <u>tackle the topic</u>.

2) The <u>middle section</u> of your essay should explain your answer in detail and give evidence to back it up. Write a <u>paragraph</u> for each point you make. Make sure you <u>comment</u> on your evidence and <u>explain how</u> it helps to <u>prove</u> your point.

3) Remember to write a <u>conclusion</u> — a paragraph at the end which <u>sums up</u> your <u>main points</u>. There's <u>more</u> about introductions and conclusions on the <u>next page</u>.

Dirk finally felt ready to tackle the topic.

To plan or not to plan, that is the question...

The answer is yes, yes, a thousand times yes. Often students dive right in, worried that planning will take up valuable time. But 5 minutes spent organising a well-structured answer is loads better than pages of waffle. Mmm waffles.

Writing Introductions and Conclusions

Now you've made that plan that I was banging on about on the last page, you'll know what your main points are. This is going to make writing your introduction and conclusion as easy as pie.

Get to the point straight away in your introduction

1) First, you need to <u>work out</u> what the question is <u>asking you</u> to do:

> **How is the character of Alfieri important to the play?**
>
> The question is <u>asking you</u> to think about the <u>role</u> of <u>Alfieri</u> in the text.
> Plan your essay by thinking about <u>how</u> this character <u>links</u> to the text's overall <u>message</u>.

2) When you've <u>planned</u> your essay, you should <u>begin</u> by giving a <u>clear answer</u> to the <u>question</u> in a sentence or two. Use the <u>rest</u> of the <u>introduction</u> to <u>develop</u> this idea. Try to include the <u>main paragraph ideas</u> that you have listed in your plan, but <u>save</u> the <u>evidence</u> for later.

3) You could also use the <u>introduction</u> to give your <u>opinion</u>. Whatever you do, make sure your introduction makes it <u>clear</u> how your answer <u>fits the question</u>.

Your conclusion must answer the question

1) The <u>most important</u> thing you have to do at the <u>end</u> of your writing is to <u>summarise</u> your <u>answer</u> to the question.

2) It's your <u>last chance</u> to persuade the examiner, so make your <u>main point</u> again.

3) Use your <u>last sentence</u> to really <u>impress</u> the <u>examiner</u> — it will make your essay <u>stand out</u>. You could <u>develop</u> your own <u>opinion</u> of the text or <u>highlight</u> which of your <u>points</u> you thought was the most <u>interesting</u>.

The examiner was struggling to see the answer clearly.

Use the question words in your introduction and conclusion

1) Try to use <u>words</u> or <u>phrases</u> from the <u>question</u> in your introduction and conclusion.

> **How does Miller use setting in the play?**

2) This will show the examiner that you're <u>answering the question</u>.

> *Miller uses setting in 'A View from the Bridge' to create symbolic meaning. The settings link to the main themes of the play, such as justice and honour.*

The first line of the introduction gives a clear answer, which will lead on to the rest of the essay.

3) This will also help you keep the question <u>fresh in your mind</u> so your answer doesn't <u>wander off-topic</u>.

I've come to the conclusion that I really like pie...

To conclude, the introduction eases the examiner in gently, whilst the conclusion is your last chance to impress. But remember — the examiner doesn't want to see any new points lurking in those closing sentences.

Writing Main Paragraphs

So we've covered the beginning and the end, now it's time for the meaty bit. The roast beef in between the prawn cocktail and the treacle tart. This page is about how to structure your paragraphs. It's quite simple...

P.E.E.D. is how to put your argument together

Remember to start a new paragraph every time you make a new point.

1) P.E.E.D. stands for: Point, Example, Explain, Develop.

2) Begin each paragraph by making a point. Then give an example from the text (either a quote or a description). Next, explain how your example backs up your point.

3) Finally, try to develop your point by writing about its effect on the audience, how it links to another part of the text or what the writer's intention is in including it.

Use short quotes to support your ideas

1) Don't just use words from the play to show what happens in the plot...

> Beatrice is upset that Eddie doesn't want her to go to Catherine's wedding — "There'll be nobody there from her family."

This just gives an example from the text without offering any explanation or analysis.

2) Instead, it's much better to use short quotes as evidence to support a point you're making.

3) It makes the essay structure clearer and smoother if most quotes are embedded in your sentences.

It's better to use short, embedded quotes as evidence. Then you can go on to explain them.

> Beatrice says that she's going to Catherine's wedding because otherwise nobody "from her family" will be there. She tries to appeal to Eddie's sense of family love — when he refuses, it shows how the Carbone family is falling apart.

Get to know some literary language

1) Using literary terms in your answer will make your essay stand out — as long as you use them correctly.

2) When you're revising, think about literary terms that are relevant to the text and how you might include them in an essay. Take a look at the table below for some examples.

Literary Term	Definition	Example
Dialect	Words from a community that are different from Standard English.	"I'm tellin' you you're walkin' wavy."
Simile	Compares one thing to another, often using 'like' or 'as'.	"his head was bouncin' like a coconut."
Metaphor	Describing something by saying it is something else.	Red Hook is "the gullet of New York".

This page is so exciting — I nearly...

Now now, let's all be grown-ups and avoid the obvious joke. It's a good way of remembering how to structure your paragraphs though. Point, Example, Explain, Develop. Simple. Maybe we could make a rap or something... anyone?

In the Exam

Keeping cool in the exam can be tricky. But if you take in all the stuff on this page, you'll soon have it down to a fine art. Then you can stroll out of that exam hall with the swagger of an essay-writing master.

Don't panic if you make a mistake

1) Okay, so say you've timed the exam beautifully. Instead of putting your feet up on the desk for the last 5 minutes, it's a good idea to <u>read through</u> your <u>answers</u> and <u>correct any mistakes</u>...

2) If you want to get rid of a mistake, <u>cross it out</u>. <u>Don't scribble</u> it out as this can look messy. Make any corrections <u>neatly</u> and <u>clearly</u> instead of writing on top of the words you've already written.

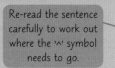

techniques
The author uses various literary ~~teknikues~~ to explore this theme .

This is the clearest way to correct a mistake. Don't be tempted to try writing on top of the original word.

3) If you've <u>left out</u> a <u>word</u> or a <u>phrase</u> and you've got space to add it in <u>above</u> the line it's missing from, write the missing bit above the line with a '^' to show exactly where it should go.

Re-read the sentence carefully to work out where the '^' symbol needs to go.

and hyperbole
The writer uses imagery to draw attention to this point.

4) If you've left out whole <u>sentences</u> or <u>paragraphs</u>, write them in a <u>separate section</u> at the <u>end</u> of the essay. Put a <u>star</u> (*) next to both the <u>extra writing</u> and the <u>place</u> you want it to go.

Always keep an eye on the time

1) It's surprisingly <u>easy</u> to <u>run out of time</u> in exams. You've got to leave <u>enough time</u> to answer <u>all</u> the questions you're asked to do. You've also got to leave enough time to <u>finish</u> each essay properly — with a <u>clear ending</u>.

2) Here are some <u>tips</u> on how to <u>avoid</u> running out of time:

- Work out <u>how much time</u> you have for each part of your answer <u>before</u> you <u>start</u>.
- Take off a few minutes at the beginning to <u>plan</u>, and a <u>few minutes</u> at the end for your <u>conclusion</u>.
- Make sure you have a <u>watch</u> to <u>time yourself</u> — and keep checking it.
- Be <u>strict</u> with yourself — if you spend <u>too long</u> on one part of your answer, you may run out of time.
- If you're <u>running out of time</u>, keep <u>calm</u>, <u>finish</u> the <u>point</u> you're on and move on to your <u>conclusion</u>.

Stephanie never had a problem with keeping cool.

Treat an exam like a spa day — just relax...

Some people actually do lose the plot when they get into the exam. The trick is to keep calm and well... carry on. If you make sure you get your exam technique sorted, you'll be as relaxed as a sloth in a room full of easy chairs.

Section Six — Exam Advice

Sample Exam Question

And now the bit you've all been waiting for — a sample exam question and a lovely little plan.
Go make yourself a cup of tea, settle down and enjoy.

Here's a sample exam question

Read this feisty exam question. That's the best way to start...

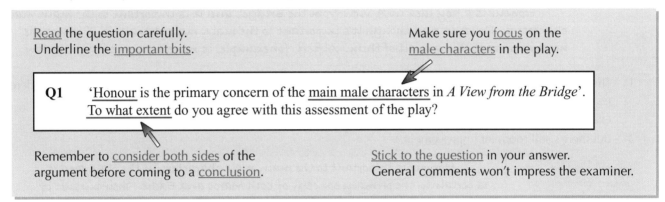

Read the question carefully.
Underline the important bits.

Make sure you focus on the
male characters in the play.

> **Q1**   'Honour is the primary concern of the main male characters in *A View from the Bridge*'.
> To what extent do you agree with this assessment of the play?

Remember to consider both sides of the
argument before coming to a conclusion.

Stick to the question in your answer.
General comments won't impress the examiner.

Here's how you could plan your answer...

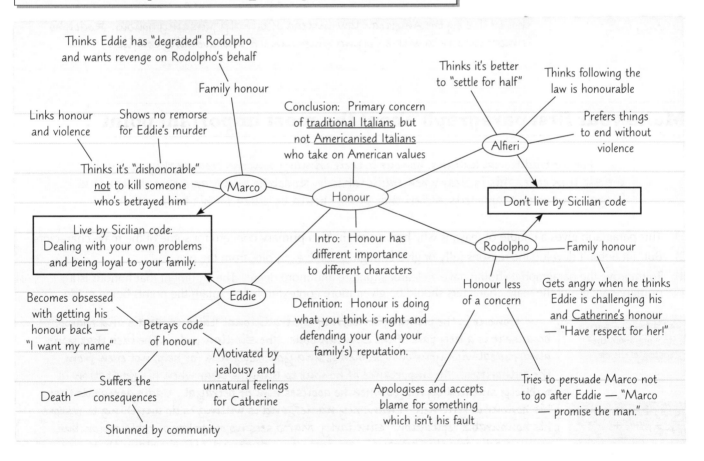

Thinks Eddie has "degraded" Rodolpho
and wants revenge on Rodolpho's behalf

Family honour

Links honour
and violence

Shows no remorse
for Eddie's murder

Thinks it's "dishonorable"
not to kill someone
who's betrayed him

Conclusion: Primary concern
of traditional Italians, but
not Americanised Italians
who take on American values

Thinks it's better
to "settle for half"

Thinks following the
law is honourable

Prefers things
to end without
violence

Alfieri

Marco

Honour

Don't live by Sicilian code

Live by Sicilian code:
Dealing with your own problems
and being loyal to your family.

Intro: Honour has
different importance
to different characters

Rodolpho

Family honour

Becomes obsessed
with getting his
honour back —
"I want my name"

Eddie

Betrays code
of honour

Definition: Honour is doing
what you think is right and
defending your (and your
family's) reputation.

Honour less
of a concern

Gets angry when he thinks
Eddie is challenging his
and Catherine's honour
— "Have respect for her!"

Death

Suffers the
consequences

Motivated by
jealousy and
unnatural feelings
for Catherine

Apologises and accepts
blame for something
which isn't his fault

Tries to persuade Marco not
to go after Eddie — "Marco
— promise the man."

Shunned by community

What do examiners eat? Why, egg-sam-wiches of course...

The most important thing to remember is DON'T PANIC. Take a deep breath, read the questions, pick a good 'un,
write a plan... take another deep breath... and start writing. Leave five minutes at the end to check your answer too.

Worked Answer

These pages will show you how to take an okay answer and turn it into a really good one that will impress the examiner.

Use your introduction to get off to a good start

These pages are all about how to word your sentences to impress the examiner, so we haven't included everything from the plan on page 59.

You might start with something like...

> Honour is a key idea in 'A View from the Bridge', and it is important to the main male characters. However, even though it's important to the main male characters, it is not the most important thing to all of them. Alfieri, for example, is more concerned with the law.

1) This intro is okay. It introduces an argument, and it shows that the importance of honour has been considered.
2) It's also a good idea to use the key words in the question to give your essay focus and show the examiner you're on track, and that you're thinking about the question from the start.
3) But there's still room for improvement...

Repeating words or phrases from the question will help focus your answer.

The examiner will give you credit for using a technical literary term.

> Honour is important to the main male characters in the play, and it is certainly the primary concern of both Marco and Eddie. Their pursuit of honour at all costs is what drives the play to its tragic conclusion. However, Miller's characterisation carefully divides the male characters into two groups. For the first group, Eddie and Marco, the traditional Italians, honour is everything. For the second group, Rodolpho and Alfieri, who have adopted American ideas, honour is not so much of a concern. Alfieri believes that people should live by the American law, instead of blindly pursuing honour. Rodolpho is more concerned with enjoying American life and avoiding conflict.

Make your first paragraph about the most important point

> For the traditional Italians, honour is their primary concern because they believe in the Sicilian code. This is clear when Eddie takes in Rodolpho and Marco even though it is illegal, and when Marco tells Alfieri that Eddie should be killed for his betrayal.

1) This paragraph gives a couple of reasons why honour might be a primary concern for some of the male characters.
2) But... it doesn't develop the reasons fully or give enough specific examples from the play.
3) To improve the paragraph it should have a clearer structure and more detail. The argument that honour is a primary concern of the male characters should be given more context to help explain the points being made.

This shows that you've thought about the context of the play.

Using quotes to back up your points shows the examiner that you know the play inside out.

> Honour is the primary concern of the traditional Italians, Eddie and Marco, because it is a key part of the Sicilian code. The Sicilian code is the idea that you always deal with your own problems, and you never ask for help, not even from the authorities. The importance of honour to Eddie is clear when his reputation is publicly smeared by Marco when he accuses him of betrayal. Eddie demands that his honour is returned: "I want my name", and is willing to do anything to restore his honourable reputation. Similarly, Marco sees no other honourable option but to kill Eddie after his betrayal. He doesn't understand Alfieri's claim that "To promise not to kill is not dishonorable". Eddie and Marco's desperate attempts to regain their honour lead to the tragic climax of the play. By the end, they both prove that they will go to any length to regain their honour.

This tells the examiner that you're thinking about the play as a whole.

Worked Answer

You need to make a variety of points

After you've explained that honour is a primary concern of some male characters, you could start your next point like this:

> For the other male characters, honour is less of a concern. This might be because their experience of American culture has altered their opinions.

1) It introduces the idea that honour might be affected if the character has been influenced by American culture.
2) However, you can make this paragraph better by giving more detailed examples and backing up points with quotes.

The more evidence you can provide, the more convincing your argument. Evidence can be a quote or a description of an event from the play.

> For Rodolpho and Alfieri, American life has altered their perspectives. Instead of believing blindly in the Sicilian code, Alfieri thinks that it is better to "settle for half". This means relying on the law to solve your problems rather than taking things into your own hands, which can lead to violence. Rodolpho's admiration for American culture and desire for peace means he places less importance on the traditional Italian view of honour. He tries to persuade Marco not to harm Eddie, and even apologises to Eddie for what has happened.

3) You could also develop it by comparing how the Americanised Italians and traditional Italians see honour.

Remember to keep referring back to the question wording to make sure that your answer is focused.

> Alfieri has been in America for a long time, so he values the American legal system more than the Sicilian code. To Alfieri, 'honour' does not mean the same thing as it does to Eddie and Marco. Alfieri's primary concern is the law. For the most part, he believes that it is honourable to follow the law, especially when blindly pursuing honour could lead to violence. This is why Alfieri tells Marco that "To promise not to kill is not dishonourable". To Alfieri, American law is more important than Italian justice.

Finish your essay in style

You could say:

> In conclusion, honour is important to all of the male characters. However, it isn't necessarily the main concern for all of them. The importance of honour to each character seems to be affected by how much they value the traditional Sicilian code.

1) This conclusion is okay but it doesn't consider exactly how important honour is to each male character.
2) So to make it really impressive you could say something like...

> Honour is important to all of the male characters, but it is not a primary concern to all of them. Honour matters to Alfieri and Rodolpho, but rather than being motivated by maintaining their reputations, Rodolpho is motivated by his love for Catherine and Alfieri by his belief in the law. However, honour is a primary concern for Eddie and Marco. In the final scenes of the play, Eddie's unnatural desire for Catherine, the driving force of the first act of the play, is replaced by his desire to regain his honour. For both Eddie and Marco it becomes all-consuming. The play's tragic ending is inevitable because they'll both do anything to protect their honour.

This focuses on the question. The word "However" shows that you're thinking about both sides of the argument.

Make your last sentence really stand out — it's your last opportunity to impress the examiner.

Why do alligators write good essays? Their quotes are snappy...

It seems like there's a lot to remember on these two pages, but there's not really. To summarise — write a good intro and conclusion, make a good range of points (one per paragraph) and put your most important point in paragraph one. Easy.

Index

The Characters from 'A View from the Bridge'

Phew! You should be an expert on *A View from the Bridge* by now. But if you want a bit of light relief and a quick recap of the play's plot, sit yourself down and read through *A View from the Bridge — The Cartoon*...

Eddie
Carbone

Beatrice
Carbone

Catherine

Rodolpho

Marco

Alfieri

Louis

Mike

Arthur Miller's 'A View from the Bridge'

ETV43